How to
Read Your
Client's Mind

How to
Read Your
Client's Mind

Kerry Johnson, MBA, Ph.D.

Published 2019 by Gildan Media LLC
aka G&D Media
www.GandDmedia.com

FIRST EDITION 2019

Front cover design by David Rheinhardt of Pyrographx

Interior design by Meghan Day Healey of Story Horse, LLC

Library of Congress Cataloging-in-Publication Data is available upon request

ISBN: 978-1-7225-0180-8

10   9   8   7   6   5   4   3   2   1

Contents

Introduction 1

One   How to Keep Someone's Attention 7

Two   Subliminal Seduction.......................................19

Three   What Their Bodies Are Telling You 33

Four   Nuances of Communication 45

Five   Persuasion as Science and Art...................... 63

Six   Eight Steps to Good Listening...................... 77

Introduction

In the mid-1970s, after I graduated from college, I walked into a San Diego employment agency looking for a job. Armed with a BA in experimental psychology, I was at a point in my life where I didn't quite know what career path to follow. Being an honor student, I was so enraptured with psychological research that I scarcely thought about where my degree would lead.

I had only a few options. I could either go on to graduate school, furthering my esoteric endeavors in obscure psychological phenomenology, or get a job. A few days after graduation, I walked into the sales office of a large computer manufacturer, trying to convince the interviewer that I had skills that could be useful to some employer somewhere.

Scanning my résumé, he looked over the top of his glasses and said flatly, "If you're an aspiring college professor, you're in great shape. Otherwise, I have a $3-an-hour job for you parking cars." Shocked, I struggled in my mind to find any research on sales or persuasive communication that would convince him that I had studied in the sales area, if not actually possessing selling experience.

I suddenly remembered a study I did as a junior on nonverbal behavior. Based on Ray Birdwhistell's book *Kinesics and Context*, my studies delved into the behavioral patterns people show when they think. I researched more than twenty other studies on the subject. I also had extensive videotaped sessions with people we had interviewed. We asked questions leading them to states of happiness, skepticism, anger, and interest, among many others. We were able to see a strong relationship between many observable body movements and the emotions the subjects reported. Describing all this research to the sales manager, I sensed his interest in picking me up. Apparently their sales training consisted of features and benefits and ten ways to close, but nothing on the behavioral side of selling.

He asked me if I'd ever spoken to a group before. I said, "Sure. Many times." I actually had only presented once before to a group of ten freshmen in an after-class meeting, but I really wanted the job.

He said, "Do you charge a fee to speak?"

I said, "Well, uh, $150." I would have felt lucky to get $25, but I thought a low price might him think I wasn't any good.

"Sounds fine," he said. "Let's schedule it for three weeks from now in San Francisco."

Boy, I was really scared. Not only had I never received a fee before, but I felt intimidated that they wanted to import me by airplane. Practicing night and day for three weeks, at twenty-two years of age, I presented my three-hour talk on nonverbal communication.

Although my speaking skills were mediocre at best, they were good enough to elicit a job offer from the manager, this time to a group of managers at the Columbia School of Broadcasting. I was very flattered by the attention, but just at that time, I received written invitations from tournament directors to play in the Grand Prix tennis circuit, so I decided to try my hot hand at professional tennis.

When I returned from the tennis tour, I turned my attention to academia, studying client relations and sales psychology in my graduate-level research. After graduation, I got experience selling as a stockbroker. I applied my PhD (piled higher and deeper) research into real-world applications.

The purpose of this book is to give you a good idea of what your listener is really thinking, sometimes in spite of what he or she says. After reading this, you should be vastly sharper with your clients, in your ability not only to read their nonverbal cues, but also to listen and persuade.

Whether you're a salesman, accountant, lawyer, or manager, you are paid to communicate with people. Your income will grow commensurately, not with your tactical ability, but with your ability to read people well enough to communicate the right message at the right time.

At a recent financial conference, the top producer, making over $1 million in commissions per year, said, "You all out there in the audience keep asking me how I analyze my clients' portfolios. I'm no better at this than you are, but I'm a great communicator. I make more money than you because I read my clients better than you. I'm paid to know how to deal with people, not to analyze their portfolios. I pay employees to do that for me."

This really shouldn't surprise you. In our age of technological thinking, we would like to think that those with the better mousetraps win. This is not always the case. Technology doesn't make money; *you* do—through the way you deal with people.

This six-chapter book is delineated into three distinct sections. The first two chapters present some basic principles. Chapters 3 and 4 provide further illustration of these concepts, but most importantly, they'll delve more deeply into the behaviors you often see in your clients but may not know why. Chapter 5, on persuasion skills, is a set of ideas that will make you much more persuasive simply because you will know the basic desires of most of your clients and how to appeal to those desires. It'll give you extra insight into how to best appeal to people. Chapter 6 suggests techniques you can use to *listen* people into accepting your ideas rather than trying to *talk* them into it.

You'll be asked to visualize numerous gestures and behaviors. I recommend that you spend a few minutes familiarizing yourself with the characteristics of each behavioral gesture.

The best way to learn this material is to read this book at least three times in the space of thirty days. Research into memory has shown that you will forget approximately 90 percent of what you hear after seven days. Through the reinforcement of rereading, that percentage will drop to 60 percent, and if you go through the book a third time, you'll retain up to 80 percent of what you've heard after thirty days.

To learn any new ideas, you must practice them. Try to use as much of what you hear as possible on your friends and acquaintances. To develop your confidence, try to apply the ideas first on them. (It'll be fun to watch your associates cross their arms, put their fingers up to their face, or sit back in their chairs.) If you use the ideas first in a nonthreatening environment, you'll be much more effective with your clients.

After you've used these techniques, send me a note. I'd like to know how you've applied the ideas. Since I write so frequently for magazines, it's very likely I'll use your experiences in my monthly columns. My contact information is:

Kerry@KerryJohnson.com
714-368-3650
Twitter: @DrKerryJohnson
Linked In: Kerry Johnson, MBA, PhD
Facebook: Kerry Johnson, MBA, PhD

One

How to Keep Someone's Attention

When you've been one-to-one with a prospect or client, have you ever gotten the impression that they didn't quite agree with something you had just said? Did they ever seem a bit skeptical with you, as if they didn't quite understand it? Or didn't believe it?

The problem is that by the time they tell you what they didn't believe or disagreed with, it's too late.

Wouldn't you love to know what people are thinking at the time they're thinking it? Let me give you an example.

Have you ever seen people move their glasses down the bridge of their nose when they're talking to you? Or have you ever seen people look over the tops of their glasses quickly? Or if they don't wear glasses, they'll look out from under their eyebrows.

These people are feeling that they disagree. They don't believe what you're saying, or they don't understand it. They want you to prove it to them on the spot. If you can prove things to your prospects exactly when they want it proven to them, you're going to keep them in agreement with you most of the time. If you can keep them in agreement with you most or all of the time, they're eventually going to do—guess what?

I did a program once for Transamerica, the life-insurance company. An agent came up to me afterwards and said, "Kerry, I see this in my prospects all the time. I know I'm in trouble when they take their glasses off and stare at me." He added, "I know I'm really in trouble when they take their contact lenses out."

When to Push

Here's a tough question. Do you think of yourself as a little bit pushy with your prospects and clients? Are you a hard closer?

Someone once asked me, "Kerry, what about these hard closers, these ex-door-to-door, Fuller Brush salesmen? They're just outmoded, aren't they?"

No, they're not, because if you can push and back off at the right time, you're going to treat them they want to be treated and sell them the way they want to be sold. There's a time and place to push your prospects hard; there's a time and place to push people very hard. Sometimes people get relationship stress: they feel uneasy talking about their money or precious resources—or just being with you causes psychological stress.

Your prospects may do two things to let you know that they're feeling pushed, closed, high-stressed. Number one, they may break eye contact for more than a couple of seconds. The second thing they may do is rub their foreheads, with or without breaking eye contact. Have you ever noticed these nuances before? You will see them today if you go sell. You bet you will.

A few years ago, I was in a church in El Paso, Texas, speaking on stress. After I was done, the minister got up and did a fifteen-minute close on his congregation. (He was an enormously popular minister, because his church had six commandments and four do-the-best-you-cans.) That minister got up and did a fifteen-minute close on his congregation that went like this: "I want all you sinners to dedicate yourself to the Lord tonight. Can I have an amen on this?"

As I looked down to the audience where that minister was pointing, I saw three people in the front row rubbing their foreheads and looking away. What are people thinking when they do this? Do they just have an itch? They're showing you that they're feeling uneasy, stressed. Basically, they're feeling they don't want to be there. What do you do?

A woman came up to me at a presentation in Toronto and said, "Kerry, I was giving a presentation on a major financial product. In the middle of the presentation, the decision maker started rubbing his forehead. I thought the guy had an itch, but then I remembered your presentation. I had to stop talking, and I said, 'I could tell you're feeling some uneasiness about this. Would you like to share your thoughts with me? I can tell this is bothering you a little bit. Would you like to tell me what you're thinking?'"

"Kerry," she said, "the point is not using these words. The point is knowing *when* to use these words."

If you can pull emotions out of your prospects and clients at the right time, they'll tell you things they wouldn't tell their spouses. They'll put that much trust in you, and when they put trust in you, suddenly you have a lifelong client rather than a one-shot customer.

Reading Signs of Boredom

Have you ever bored anybody? Here's a nugget for you. When your prospects are bored, they're likely not listening. Why waste your time? It's much too precious.

We have done three years of research on what your prospects do when they're listening to you talk. We have noticed that when they do the things I'm about to show you, they'll retain about 10 percent of the message one hour afterwards. I call that wasting your time. Don't you?

There are two reasons why your prospects or clients get bored. Number one: they were interested in what you're talking about, but they aren't any longer, because you spent too long talking about it. Number two: they never cared in the first place. Correct?

One of my graduate professors at the University of California in San Diego said, "Kerry, I know you're going to be doing a lot of speaking around the country. You have to realize one thing: the audience is only listening to you for 10 percent of the time you speak. Another 20 to 30 percent of the time, they're thinking about their own personal problems and frustrations. The other 60 percent of the time, they're having sexual fantasies. I'll tell you, it's nice for me to know that for almost two-thirds of our meeting time, you're having fun."

Here is the most obvious boredom signal on the face of the earth.
It's tapping your fingers—thumping.
I call it the SOS boredom signal. How
many times have you seen people that
drum their fingers on the table in front of

you or on their knee? I hate to see this. If I'm speaking to a group
of 200, and there is one person doing this, I change my talk, and I
change it drastically, because I know that other people are probably
bored too.

Clickers and Tappers

Probably the most common things,
though, are what people do with
pencils and pens. Like the ball-
point-pen clicker. The more bored
they get, the faster they click.

Before Jimmy Fallon on *The Tonight Show* was Johnny Carson.
Johnny was the king of boredom. Johnny got bored so often, he had
a pencil specially made for it. It had an eraser on both ends. You
could almost always tell when he was bored. He'd tap his pencil on
his desktop whenever his sidekick, Ed McMahon, started talking. I
remember watching the show once. Ed was talking,
Johnny was tapping. After about four or five minutes, Johnny starting doing little finger trills. I
never knew his fingers could move that quickly.
One minute before the commercial came
on, Johnny got so bored he was watching the eraser hit his desktop.

There was an actor called Charles Nelson Reilly. He had a machine-gun mouth. If you asked him how's the weather, he'd be off talking about Topanga Canyon, his house, the work that he was doing right now, his next book. He was just an extremely boring person, and obviously Johnny thought he was boring too, because as soon as Reilly started talking, Johnny started tapping.

Here are some more boredom signals. In most cases when your male prospects or clients are sitting with you, they will typically will have their legs crossed very widely, with the ankle on the knee. When they have come to the end of their boredom rope, they'll do tap-dance boredom signals. They'll start moving their feet up and down from their ankles. The more bored they get, the faster that foot goes.

Women are much more elegant at this than males are. When women come to the end of their boredom rope, they will typically do what I call rotation boredom. They will start moving their feet in circular motions. Or they will move their legs from the knee up, whereas men usually move their feet up and down from the ankle. Some women, when they have their legs crossed, will tap the bottom of a table, or they'll tap the floor.

Boredom is also seen when people slouch in their chairs, and when they doodle. People that give you blank expressions are certainly bored. When my son Neal was around seven, he was throwing rocks at girls, and I tried to cure him of that. I had a talk with him for about five minutes one day, and I said, "Neal, girls have neat equipment. It could be damaged. Don't throw rocks. Be nice to them, because Santa told me that."

After I talked to him for about five minutes, he had his head in his hands. I said, "Now, Neal, do you understand everything I've been talking to you about girls and not throwing rocks?"

He gave me that blank look, and he said, "Dad, how many teeth do you have?" Really paying attention, right? Really understood what I was talking about.

The most typical sign of boredom is when people rest their head in their hands. I get the feeling that they're about to nod off. This is what I call the lullaby boredom. This is the worst type that you can encounter.

Yawning—that's another one. Sure—go to lunch.

How to Eradicate Boredom

Here's how to eradicate boredom from all your prospects from now on. Simple, but yet very easy to apply. Never again talk for more than thirty seconds at a time without saying to person you're talking to, "Any comments about this? Anything you'd like to add? Anything you'd like to say?"

As human beings, we only have an intense attention span of only thirty seconds. (Ever wonder why television commercials are only thirty seconds long?) If you talk for more than thirty seconds at a time, your prospect starts to think of questions they'd love to ask you, comments they would love to make. After thirty seconds, they start to think about what they want to say rather than what you're saying. They're thinking about what they want to say after you're done talking. So get the person to talk as much as you can. Selling is not talking. Selling is listening.

How about the telephone? Do you still smile and dial? This time it's fifteen seconds for attention span. Obviously, you can't see them face-to-face, but if you don't get feedback every fifteen seconds, you have typically lost that call. (Unless the person is an incredibly good friend of yours. Then they might bear it).

Four Steps to Presentation Success

Here's a four-step technique on making your presentations so impactful, so emotion-committing, that the people who listen to you will not only retain more of what you say, but will be more inspired to do what you'd like them to do. Ready for this?

Do one of these four things every four to five minutes.

1. Start out by asking a rhetorical question, and then pause.
2. Use a story from your own personal experience. People want to hear how you've lived what you're talking about.
3. Use a quick, humorous, one-liner anecdote to cap off every major idea. Researchers at San Diego State University showed that if you use humor, people will remember and retain more of what you say.
4. This is probably the most important part: get physical participation from the group. Ask people to do things or say something to the person next to them.

Here's the fifth, bonus point: never present more than four to five major ideas at any one sitting.

Using these techniques the right way will make up for a lack of speaker talent.

The Power of Touch

Would you like your prospects and clients to understand three times as much in one-half the time? Then pay close attention.

Remember when you were young and mom and dad said, "Don't point to things, Murray. It's not nice." Thank goodness you ignored that advice, because the research has shown that you have to do the things you were taught not to do. Point to concepts or ideas you want to flag. Keep your finger on it while you talk. Sales managers, this will be useful to keep attention and underline ideas. Research has now shown that if your prospects cannot see an idea or concept for a minimum of twenty to thirty seconds, it may not go into long-term memory, which means it's likely to be forgotten within twenty to thirty minutes.

Here's a similar point. A number of years ago, two researchers did a project in which they took a quarter and put it on a ledge next to a telephone into a phone booth. Then they walked out of the booth and hid behind a tree.

Most people would pick up a quarter lying by itself in an empty phone booth, and that's what people did in this experiment. They would walk out with the quarter. The researchers would go up to the culprits and say, "Did you happen to see my quarter in that phone booth? I have to make another phone call. Did you happen to see that when you were in there?"

The researchers found that only 23 percent of the time did the subject give back the quarter.

On the other hand, these researchers were very bright guys. They did something a little bit different. This time they replaced the quarter, hid behind a tree, and waited for another subject to walk in and walk out, but when they came up the subject, they touched him or her on the side of the arm for less than three seconds. Then they said, "Sir, did you happen to see my quarter in there?"

In the majority of these cases, the subjects would reach in their pockets and say, "Son of a gun, is this your quarter? I was just looking for someone to give it back to."

Quick question. During the last twenty-four hours, in your social life, without even knowing it, did you ever touch somebody on the side of the arm to grab their attention, reinforce a comment, or underline something you thought was important for them to know? Do you have any idea how effective this is in getting people to make decisions, in closing customers, making them commit or stop procrastinating?

A gentlemen who sells financial products in Lansing, Michigan, wrote me a letter and said, "Kerry, it's incredible. I was with one guy in Michigan for a long time, about nine months. I couldn't seem to get the guy to buy. I guess I didn't say the right things, although I kept going back in and saying different things all the time. I guess trust wasn't very high. Something was going wrong.

"Kerry, I used your technique when I tried to close him last time. I was going to give up on him, but I used your technique, and I touched him. All I know is I walked out of that office with a check for $6,000. I got a whole lot of commission out of that, from a technique that I did not normally use. Even though I considered it common sense, I was not applying it in common practice, but I now have made it into common money."

Sometimes it's the simple things that you're currently not doing that will work the best in your business.

Two

Subliminal Seduction

You're being seduced almost every single day by almost every part of your environment. Las Vegas has known for years how to seduce you. Las Vegas has known for a long time that if they lower their lights to hypnotic levels, they will entrance you (they call it "entrancing" rather than "entrapping"). Las Vegas will never have a clock or windows in any casino. Why? Because they don't want you to know what time it is.

You'll never see a slot machine by itself in a casino. You'll only see slot machines in groups of four, five, or six. Why? Because Las Vegas wants you to hear the money coming down the chute on the slot machines that you're not using. "This thing is going to hit any second; all the others are. How come mine isn't?" They want you to pivot and put a quarter in that one.

Kmart is now using similar technology. Kmart has been lowering their lights to hypnotic levels too (which they also call "entrancement"). Kmart has learned how to put Muzak on. They've also learned how to make blue lights flash around to captivate small minds.

Kmart has now learned something interesting about the Muzak, or mood music. Now we've known in industrial psychology that Muzak will increase worker performance and decrease worker tension. Kmart has learned a technique about putting soundtracks below that Muzak. Subliminally, unconsciously, you can hear it, but not consciously. Now it does it over and over again, during all store hours. "Please don't steal. We want you to buy, buy, buy."

In the thirteen months after introducing this subliminal messaging, Kmart said their shoplifting had gone down by 46 percent. Kmart also said their consumption increased by 19 percent more than expectations in the same time frame.

What are the first three words our children learn when they're young these days? "Attention, Kmart shoppers."

Twelve Seductive Words

According to research from Yale University, there are twelve words that are the most subliminally seductive. If you're doing direct mail, these twelve words will get you a better response. You can also use these words in one-to-one, written correspondence to give the recipient more retention of what you write. In fact, you'll be more easily persuaded to use these words yourself, because they will help your prospects remember and be more easily persuaded.

Discovery	New
Easy	Proven
Guaranteed	Results
Health	Safety
Love	Save
Money	You

Where have you heard these words most often? In the media. You see them on television. You hear them on the radio. Newspapers have been using them for quite a while.

You may have been using these tools without even knowing it. You just say, "Hey, these words sound like they're good to use. Let's just use them. We'll see what happens," and you test them against other things. That's what market research is about—trying to turn common sense into analytical reality.

These things typically will work. The problem is that they become very manipulative. They'll be used by other people on you. (They become *very* manipulative if your spouse uses them on you.)

The Handshake

One of the first greetings you give anybody is a handshake. They really are nuances to this, but they can mean a lot.

Gentlemen, at five years old, you learned how to shake hands the right way. Basically, your father walked up to you and said, "Now, son, I want to teach you a good, firm, solid, business handshake. Tough handshake. Shake like a man."

What about those people who don't give you that good, firm, solid, tough, business handshake? What about those people who

give you something else—the
limp-fish, that wet-noodle handshake? A few people will shake
your fingertips and don't quite
squeeze. Then there are the ones who shake
your hands for a few minutes but let you know they're losing interest because they start looking away in the middle of the handshake.

These people are showing you something you cannot ignore in
business. They're often showing you low self-esteem, low self-confidence, what we psychologists call low levels of assertiveness.
They're showing you they don't like to make decisions very quickly
or make commitments very fast. If you're a realtor, they may take
three months to go for a nothing-down property with positive
cash flow.

I beg you, please, to push these people a lot harder than you
would anybody else, because they may be wasting your time. You've
heard of closing? I think you should close these people hard.

Sometimes you hear it said that you should never close. Is that
right? No—these people you should close. Use it as a tool, because
20 percent of the people that you come in contact with give you
about 80 percent of your business. I treat the other 80 percent the
right way—the way they want to be treated. You sell them the way
they want to be sold, not the way you want to sell them.

Can you tell much about somebody—their personality, their
characteristics, their attitudes, their image, their behavior—just by
the way they look? Take the kind of guy who dresses very sharp.
His shoes match his pants, his jacket. Everything about him looks
impeccable. A guy like this is showing he has a high degree of tradi-
tionality, a high level of establishment attitude. He uses the business
handshake, the establishment handshake.

Well, buckaroo, times are changing. We have a lot of high-tech whiz kids these days. They come to work in Frank Zappa T-shirts and Levi's they haven't washed in four weeks, but they have tons of money. The problem is, they don't want to shake your establishment hand like your grandfather. They want to shake hands like they were in the 'hood twenty years ago. This is handshake at a forty-five-degree angle, done in a way that draws you in. The problem is, you never know when this is coming up. Sometimes you go up to these young Turks. Sometimes you miss.

Do you ever miss when you shake hands with people? Do you ever walk up to somebody and just grab their fingertips? Do you ever grab their fingertips by mistake and just stand there feeling embarrassed? Or get so excited that you found a prospect who already wants what you've got that your fingers go up the poor guy's sleeve?

Leonard Zunin wrote a book called *Contact: The First Four Minutes.* He said that we make more than 93 percent of lasting impressions in the first four minutes, and I couldn't agree more with that. There are hundreds of ways to apply this, but one way is, if you ever miss, if you walk up to somebody and grab their fingertips by mistake, regain that handshake back quickly, within the first four minutes.

Let's face it. A lot of women give you that little, wimpy ex-housewife handshake. In fact a lot of males 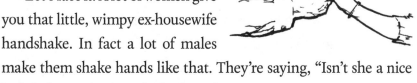 make them shake hands like that. They're saying, "Isn't she a nice little lady? Go back to the keyboard."

You know how this started out? Going back to the eighteenth century, women would offer their hands to be kissed.

Ladies, would you like a little bit more respect from males with your strengths and abilities as a professional? Nuances are crucially important. From now on, ladies, I want you to command that extra respect from males. Shake their hand so that your palm touches their palm. Also, shake their hand so that your fingers are wrapped around their hand.

Males often think it's important for a woman to offer her hand first before they shake hands with her. Women don't care who shakes hands first in business, just so you shake hands. So, gentlemen, these days you may run the risk of insulting a woman unless you offer your hand to her as an equal decision maker. If you don't shake hands with a woman in the way she wants you to (instead of the way your father taught you to), you may insult her professional dignity.

Heed Buying Signals

Why not sell your product when your prospect wants to buy it instead of when you want to sell it?

Isn't that incredibly obvious? But have you ever oversold anybody by talking way too long? Have you talked about something your prospect didn't even care about, but you felt you had to say it?

Do your prospects tell you when they want to be closed? Do they say, "Hold it, I'm ready. Close me quick. Hurry"? Does that happen in your business? Me neither.

If it doesn't happen like that, watch for these specific cues, because your prospects will let you know exactly when they want to buy, and if you don't let them, you're going to oversell them, or you're not going to get any business at all.

Number one, your prospects will typically nod their head and smile at you a whole lot more than when they first came into the room with you. If you didn't know this, you shouldn't be in business. But did you also know that the faster they nod their heads when they're listening to you, the more they're thinking, "I wish this clown would shut up"?

Another buying signal that you'll typically see, even when the room is very bright, is that pupils will dilate during periods of heavy excitement and enthusiasm.

Let me prove it to you. Your kids came out from their rooms on Christmas Day. They saw all those presents around the tree. They said, "Mommy, Daddy, is that for me?" Their eyebrows went up to the sky. Did you watch their pupils do the same thing?

If you've ever played poker, you seen that guy who's wearing sunglasses. Why? He has a full house.

What do your prospects do with the things that you've given them to look at? Do they give them back to you? Do they put them on your side of the table? Do they push them away? They're showing psychological "dispossessiveness." They're showing that the idea is not that important. The need is not that high. Trust is very low. Go back, and do better probing. Find out what they really want before you even try to close.

On the other hand, do they take that sheet of paper? Do they look at it for a couple of seconds or a couple of minutes? Do they put it on their side of the table, their side of the desk? Do they say, "Is this my copy?"

If they love what they're seeing and hearing, be careful. Don't oversell. You'll buy it back.

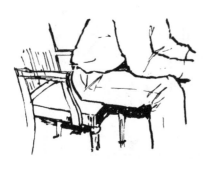

The most common buying signal you'll ever see is called the whistling teapot. Imagine a teapot that wants to buy so badly it wants to explode. The prospect will lean forward in their chair, or sit on the edge of your chair. This is an incredibly good buying signal.

Have you ever had anybody buy products from you sitting back in their chair, crossing their arms, crossing their legs, breaking eye contact? Does that happen much in your business? More often, don't they lean forward in their chair when they're about to make major purchases?

Do this now: Keep sitting forward. Put your left hand on your left knee. Put your right forearm on your right thigh. This is a great buying signal, and if you can't close them in this position, try Avon.

Listen to this true story. A gentleman from Lansing, Michigan, wrote me a letter and said, "Kerry, I sold a financial product, which netted me $10,000 in two meetings. It was incredible. During the first meeting with one of the prospects, a business owner, I was probing him, getting information. The second day, when I did the presentation, he started doing that sitting tremor position that you talked about. He leaned forward in his chair with his right hand on his right knee and left hand on his left thigh.

"Kerry, I saw it happening. I had to stop talking, and I decided to close him. I did an assumptive close. I took that business owner out to dinner that night and asked, 'What made you want to buy so quick? I expected it to take a lot longer. What did I say that moti-vated you so much?' The prospect said, 'Partner, I was ready to go for that idea one hour before you stopped talking.'"

Think of the business you're losing by overselling, overtalking, overdoing it.

Proxemics

I'm going to give you a technique right now for getting higher trust, higher warmth, in five minutes than you previously could in two weeks. It will get you more trust, not from what you say, but from the way you sit.

The science of personal space is called *proxemics*. You probably know that the closer your prospect is to you, standing or sitting, the more warmth and trust they feel for you. The farther they are away from you, sitting down or standing up, the worse they tend to feel about you. Pretty common-sense stuff.

There's something called the *intimacy distance*. It's zero to one foot away. You should use it only for the most intimate of your clients or prospects. This is the most emo-tionally charged distance you can be at. The only problem is, if you're here for more than about three seconds, it suddenly turns into a distance that's only reserved for male-female relationships. So be very careful after three seconds.

The next one is not quite so obvious. It's called the *friendship distance*. This is between one and two feet away. People stand at this distance when they like and feel comfortable with each other. If you're meeting a person for the first time, you take a step forward, reach in to this distance, and say, "Hi. My name is Kerry Johnson. What's your name?" Then you move back to a more normal security distance.

To help your client feel more comfortable, go into that person's friendship space. If you use, say, a comp analysis sheet, you can say, "I just wanted you to look at this. Look at all the values in the properties around here. Are they within your price range?"

I show the sheet to him. I point at things of interest; then I give it to him, and I back up just a step while staying in his friendship space. If he does not take a step back, I know that he feels comfortable with me.

Two to three feet away is called the *acquaintance distance.* The acquaintance distance is reserved for people who don't know each other, although they meet at a common ground, say a conference or a party.

Three feet and beyond is called the *stranger distance.* If I had my druthers, I would druther stand this far away from the next person at the movie theater or a bus stop, or in line.

There are individuals that sit across the table from you, with long distances in between. When you first went into business, isn't it true that you had a desk that had no overhang, no lip, at all, just straight up and down? Then we graduate to getting an office. When we have done a couple of million-dollar months, then we get a secretary. Then the pièce de résistance—the desk that has a lip on it. Finally, you know you're important, because you're able to keep people farther away. In offices, the size of the overhang, or the lip,

on a desk says a lot about how
important that person is. Some
individuals use this kind of territo-
riality to keep their distance from
you. It's a sign of overconfidence.

If you have a client come into your office, *never* sit behind your
desk. From now on, I want you to sit right in front, bring that guy
right in front of your desk, and have a chat. You're going to have
higher rapport, more trust, more quickly than you ever could from
behind your desk. After all, what do you do when you see friends?
Friends come over to your house. Do you sit across the living room?
Of course you don't. You sit right next to them on the couch. Simi-
larly, when you're sitting down with your client at a table, don't sit
across the table. Sit next to the person. It adds a lot to their comfort
and to how well you can persuade them. Because what happens when
we're comfortable with somebody? We trust them, empathy goes up,
and suddenly the relationship causes us to feel better about them.

The same holds true for managers. If a subordinate or a peer
comes into your office, make sure that you don't sit behind your
desk. You're just telling them, "I'm more important than you are.
Don't get too close to me." Come out from behind your desk. It'll do
a lot to raise the comfort level.

Sometimes you go into other people's offices. You can't walk
behind that guy's desk and say, "Hey, some psychologist told me to
sit next to you. Hope you don't mind." But here is a great technique
that I think will work for you.

Typically the person will greet you at his door. He will come up,
say, "Hi," and shake hands.

What I want you to do from now on is say, "Jack, I have a couple
of things I want to talk to you about. I don't want to read these upside

down across your desk. Do you mind if we sit in these two chairs over here? I just don't want to crick my neck. Is that all right with you?"

He wants to help you. Give it a try.

Another thing related to proxemics: there's a line of demarcation, a separation point, right smack-dab in the middle of any interaction you have, any distance you have with somebody.

Let me tell you about an experiment that we did when I was a graduate student at UC San Diego. We would go into a restaurant that had counters and chairs that had the unique non-capability of moving around. You couldn't pick them up. They couldn't move from side to side. They couldn't move up and back. They would only swivel.

We would go up to a guy who was sitting there, eating by himself with the newspaper. We'd sit down, and of course, he knew we were here. We'd order a hamburger, a glass of milk, and a cup of coffee.

The milk would come. We'd take a little sip of the milk, and put it right smack-dab on that line of demarcation, that separation point. Of course we'd always get the guy's attention. He'd look at it and look back at his paper.

We would get the coffee, take a little sip, and put it on *his* side of the milk. Funny thing was, the chair wouldn't move, but he would.

Then we would take the hamburger, take a couple of bites out of it, put a little salt on it, and then put the salt on the other side. While we had the salt in the air, the person would see it coming, and start eating away from us, in his lap. People will do anything to preserve that space.

Do you feel a little nervous in crowded elevators with a lot of people? Here's another experiment we did at the University of California, San Diego, about proxemics in elevators.

If you're a normal person, most likely you will walk into an elevator, turn around, and face the door. As researchers, we would walk into crowded San Diego bank-building elevators and *not* turn around.

You can imagine what these people were thinking: "Who the h*** is this guy?" I never saw people move so quickly away from us with a minimum of body motion. They just sort of slid.

On the last day of the project, one of my graduate students faced the wrong way in a very crowded elevator. I was in the back, making notes and giggling. He faced that way for a long time, until the elevator got very cold, very tense, and very quiet. He said something that I will never forget in my life: "I'll bet you've all wondered why I called this meeting today." Whatever button those people pushed when they got in the elevator, they all got off on the next floor.

Here's an important point. *Your prospects don't care how much you know until they first know how much you care.* When they find out you care, they want to know all that you know.

Let me tell you one quick story in closing. I happen to have been raised by my grandfather. He was the light of my life. Everything I have is because of my grandfather. He was a little old Irishman who used to say things as he'd tuck me into bed: "Kerry, I hope the rain falls gently on your fields. I hope the wind is always against your back, and until I wake you up, I hope the Lord holds you in the hollow of His hand." I loved that man a lot.

When I was thirteen years old, my grandfather died. That ripped me apart. My grandmother told me about it. She said, "Kerry, one of the last things your grandfather said was, 'Tell Kerry I'm pulling for him.'"

I sincerely care about you, and I'm pulling for you. Use these techniques. Would you, please?

Three

What Their Bodies Are Telling You

I grew up in a little town south of Portland, Oregon, called Milwaukie. Ever heard of Milwaukie? A little, tiny place. Milwaukie was a great place for a kid to grow up in. When I was ten years old, it was a wonderful place. It had a couple of farms around.

I had a good friend, whose name was Butch. We were very close, but Butch wasn't the brightest kid around. Butch was a couple of bricks shy of a load.

One farmer had a blacksmith's shop, in which he used to hammer out horseshoes and get them white-hot to texture them and shape them, because he used to shoe his own horses.

Butch and I walked into that blacksmith's shop one day, and Butch grabbed a hot horseshoe that the farmer had put out to the side to cool. You can imagine the pain he must have been in. He put it down extremely quickly. Just then, the farmer compassionately looked at him and said, "That burn you, Butch?"

Butch said, "No, sir. It just doesn't take me long to look at a horseshoe."

It didn't take me long to realize that hidden communication was important. It's so important that when I talk to people these days, I never do anything at all without recognizing these hidden forms of communication and using them as I'm talking.

How to Tell if They're Listening

When I'm doing my consulting and industrial psychology work, clients will ask me, "Kerry, how do I know if someone's listening to me? How do I know if they're paying attention?" Usually when people are listening and paying attention, they will put their finger up on the side of their face, and the thumb beneath the chin. It's more of an ambivalent gesture when they have the forearm to the side of the face and the thumb beneath the chin, although they're still listening.

On the more negative side is something I call the *seven-year itch*. If they don't quite agree with you, they might scratch the side of their head really slowly. This means that they're a little bit critical too. They're actually thinking, "Come on. Don't give me that."

What if the guy actually has an itch? If the person really has an itch, they usually put their finger up to the side of their face and they'll rub it very quickly and drop their hand. If they're evaluating what you're saying with a critical mind, they'll rub their face very slowly.

Something else is what I call the Leaning Tower of Pisa. The great naturalist Charles Darwin found that when he held a bunch of bananas up in front of a chimpanzee, the chimp would move his head from side to side, as if thinking, "What do I have to do for those bananas?" It was a sign of intense interest. If

the listener cocks their head to the side, they like what you have to say; they're very interested in what you're talking about. Keep going with these individuals.

Sometimes people who are thinking about what we have to say might say, "Hmm." They might do something like, "Huh, that's interesting," and stroke their chin. Usually they're showing us that they're thinking about what we have to say, but sometimes they do this out of ignorance. I'll give you an example.

I am a member of the American Psychological Association. Recently I got a chance to go to a meeting down in San Diego. A group of us met in the back of the banquet room before the general meeting started. While we were speaking about current issues of the day, in came a psychiatrist. He opened the door, closed it, went in, and joined the group, only hearing a few words. He said, "I don't what's wrong with that woman. She has deference subliminal dysfunction, so she's probably orally despondent." None of us knew a thing about what he was talking about, so we starting stroking our chins. "Is that so?"

People use this sometimes as a smokescreen too. Have you ever tried to explain something complex to someone? You say, "Do you understand?" They say, "Oh, yes, sure. Right, right," as they're stroking their chin. It's a camouflage technique. It's a smokescreen that people put up to keep you from knowing that no, they don't understand. If you see people doing this, get them to talk to you about it. Make sure that they understand before you go on to your next step.

What about those people that put things in their mouths when you talk to them? Ever notice that? Like putting their glasses in their mouth? Twirling their glasses around, putting their pens in their mouth.

Car salesmen say they hate to sell to teen-agers, old ladies, and people that put things in their mouth, because they never seem to make a decision. You say, "How do you like this?" They might say, "Hmm," or rather, in goes the pen.

"I notice you like this house, and you told me that this is good financing on this house. It's something you really want. Would you like to make an offer on it today?" In goes the pen. In goes the pipe. Pipes are great, aren't they? When people have pipes, they use them as a cover. Anytime they don't want to answer a question, in goes the pipe.

Mom and Dad said don't talk with your mouth full when you were young, right? So when somebody asks a question you don't want to answer, in goes the pipe, in goes the pen, in goes the glasses, because guess what? Mom told me not to talk with my mouth full, so I'm not going to talk.

Watch out for people that put things in their mouth, because this is usually a stalling technique. In this case, do a little bit more to explain the financing plan on the house. Do a little more to explain the house in general—what the appreciation might be, the comp analysis—and when they take the thing out of their mouth, stop talking, because they're ready to say something to you. Hopefully it's positive.

Openness Gestures

We frequently talk with our hands. We say, "This house is over here, and look at that properly. Isn't it beautiful? I'm glad you came in my office today," and throw our hands out.

People show openness and cooperation with open-handed gestures. They throw their hands out. They show the palms of their hands as they're speaking to you: "I've been working with a lot of agents and a lot of companies, but to tell you the truth, I want to buy my house through you."

You can manipulate people's attention by doing the right things as you're talking with your hands. Let me give you an example.

The Reverend Robert Schuller in Garden Grove, California, the Crystal Cathedral, used to have a TV ministry on Sunday mornings; millions of people watched. He would get up in his robes and never uses any visual aids, yet he commanded the attention of millions of people every single Sunday. He did it through hand signals and openness, the greatest visual aid you could ever use.

He would get up in his long robes, and he would throw his robes back. He'd say, "What the mind can conceive and believe, it will achieve," and he did this through his whole talk. I can't picture anybody in that audience who didn't give him direct attention during the half hour he was up there.

Open your hands up as you speak to people. It'll enhance openness. If you see people speaking like that, they're being very open, and what's more, they're being comfortable with you.

Here's another openness gesture. I call it "give me a break." You might work with a mortgage rep. You go to the guy and say, "Jim, why? How come this guy didn't qualify for the loan? He makes $100,000 a year. You told me there's no problem with him qualifying."

"Well, interest rates went up."

"Come on. Why don't you work for this?"

The mortgage rep says, "Give me a break. I did all I could. Come on." He puts his hands up, and the elbows are together. The palms are facing forward and up. The person is actually giving you a submissive type of openness gesture. He's being very open with you, is being very, very honest with you.

Remember the first *Godfather* movie? It had a great example of this. Six months after Don Vito Corleone was shot, the five Mafia families in New York got together to try to make a truce to iron out a problem with the drug trade. At the end of this, Barzini looked at the two and said, "Are you ready to make up?"

Don Vito Corleone looked at Tattaglia, the man widely accused of having Corleone shot. Corleone stood up out of his chair, and he went like this. He walked over to the end of the table and of course Tattaglia came over to the table, and they grabbed each other. Then they sat down.

It was a great gesture. Each knew exactly what the other meant. Openness, submissiveness. I'm burying the hatchet; no more problems with us.

At Ease

Another one is a gesture which I fondly call "at ease." How many times have you felt a little bit uncomfortable with people that come into your office? They have a tie. They have a vest on, their jackets are buttoned like this, and they walk upright. Have you ever noticed that?

These individuals are definitely not at ease. They're not showing you openness, and there's sometimes a problem getting through this barrier they're putting up. If these individuals don't at least unbutton their jacket when they sit down with you and talk, probably they are either not comfortable with you or suspicious of you. Obviously they're not very open. Sometimes they might feel a little bit defensive.

To get that person comfortable with you, make sure that you spend enough time talking about him, about his family, about what he wants, in order to get him to feel comfortable with you enough to not have to button his jacket up, not have to have his vest buttoned all the way up to his neck.

I went to a party recently, and a gentleman and I were having a drink together and talking. The hostess was an extremely shapely, beautiful woman. She came over to us, and of course refilled our drinks. As she did, my friend loosened his tie a little bit, then he unbuttoned the top button and the next two buttons on his shirt. Then she walked away.

After about twenty minutes, the hostess came back and started to refill our drinks again. As she was, the gentleman took his tie totally off and unbuttoned the rest of the buttons on his shirt. I walked away, because I was afraid if she came back again, I didn't

know what he'd lose. A good example of people showing great openness when they feel comfortable.

Here's a key. If somebody comes into your office with his jacket
and vest buttoned, and his tie looks as if it's choking him, be sure
that you spend enough time developing rapport in order to get him
to feel comfortable. Typically, we find these individuals on the East
Coast, New York. West Coast people tend to wear open shirts.

Also, if somebody comes into your office, or if you go on a showing, with somebody whose ties is unbuttoned, maybe even has the
top button unbuttoned, and no buttons buttoned on their jacket,
please don't make the mistake of having your coat buttoned, your
vest buttoned, your tie up to here.

How many of you saw *Evita*? All about Eva Perón. Eva Perón was
married to Juan Perón, who was in power in Argentina. Juan Perón
got up to speak in front of some striking workers, who were about to
rampage in rebellion. Before he got up, Eva took his jacket off him,
took his tie off, loosened his shirt down, and rolled up his sleeves,
because she knew that if he went up looking like the aristocracy in
his suit, the workers would not identify with him.

It's the same thing when you're working with a client that has
his tie loosened a little bit. Don't let yourself be impeccably dressed
either, so you can get acceptance.

Readiness

Here are some buying signals so you'll know if someone's ready to
buy. How do I know if someone's ready to make a decision, ready
for action? These individuals do little things to let you know that
they're ready. As I mentioned earlier, they sit on the edge of their
chairs while you're talking. If you're in the final phases of the selling

and you're about ready to ask them to make an offer, these people will grab the pen from you. They'll tell you what they want and how much they're willing to go for.

Another thing people do to show you this readiness is put their hands on their hips. Have you seen this before? It's good example of readiness. I call this goal-directedness.

Let me repeat a caution from earlier. Whether the person is ready to buy, whether it's a buying signal, or whether it merely means that the person wants to speed you up, realize that you can easily bore this person if you spend too long talking. If you're not in the process of closing, if you're not in the process of getting that person to make an offer, start moving on to another subject, because they're probably beginning to be a little bit bored and antsy.

Once a friend of mind decided that he was ready to buy a Cadillac Seville. He walked into a Cadillac showroom with his wife, went to the car, and put his foot on it. He said to his wife, "Isn't this a gorgeous-looking car?" He looked at it with his hands on his hips.

A salesman came out of an office that had other salesmen in it. He said, "Sir, can I help you?"

With his hands on his hips, my friend looked at the man and said, "To tell you truth, I'm very interested in this Cadillac. It's a gorgeous car, and I'd like to take a test drive."

The salesman said, "Sir, can you come back tomorrow morning? We're having a sales meeting right now."

My friend said, "Fine."

He took his wife by the arm, went six blocks down the street to another Cadillac dealership, signed on the dotted line, and drove a Seville away that day.

People with their hands on their hips are either trying to speed you up, or they're trying to say, "Yes, I like it." "Yes, I want to buy it." "Yes, I want to make an offer." "Yes, I want to do something to consummate this deal."

Another posture that people do to show interest is lean forward in the chair and put the left elbow on the left knee, and the right hand on the right knee. Ever see people sitting on the edge of their chair? This is called sit-down readiness. If a person likes a property, is interested in the  financing, wants to make an offer, and you know they can afford the house, they do this sort of thing. These people are really interested. They're almost ready to burst out and say, "Yes, that's what I want."

The Nuances of Steepling

Confident people are the very decisive individuals that you work with. They come to you and say, "I want a four-bedroom house. I want three and a half baths. I want an acre of property zoned for horses." You show them about three or four houses that fit that category and are in their price range, and they say, "Yes, that's it. That's what I want." As long as it's within the right price range, they'll make an offer on the property right then and there, because you've shown them what they want.

These people don't have to call mom and dad in Ohio to find out if New Mexico is a good place to buy property. They don't have to talk to the next-door neighbor to find out if they're dealing with a reputable firm. These are the type of people also that do a very interesting gesture, which I call steepling. A steeple is when both hands are joined at the fingertips low across the lap or higher with their chin resting on their fingers.

People that are very confident and
decisive tend to do steepling gestures. People either steeple low or they steeple high,
but the higher the steeple, the higher the
confidence level.

It's more difficult, but we do see people
steepling when they don't have a table in
front of them. When they do, they'll either
rest their hands on the table or put their
elbows on it. When they're standing up,
they'll usually steeple at about belt level.

This is a sign of high confidence, even overconfidence—
cockiness. A highly cocky person who steeples with his fingers
touching high next to his chest might say, "You want to know how
much money I make? Guess." Ego spreads like a virus in these individuals. Sometimes we need to be consultants or counselors instead
of salespeople with them, because it's usually managers and execu-
tives who have a high degree of self-esteem.

A male will usually steeple at chest height, but women most often
steeple low in their lap, This is called *subtle steepling*, and it shows a
competent confidence. Women are just as confident as males are,
but they don't do things as overtly. Often they will clench one hand
into a fist, with the other hand covering the fist. I get a little bit nervous when I'm around a woman that does this. I feel she's thinking,
"Get any closer to me, buddy, and I'll punch you."

Four

Nuances of Communications

What I've been telling you so far has been oriented toward WASPs: white Anglo-Saxon Protestants. But these days we have a lot of diversity. We have Hispanics and Asians. A lot of these gestures that I'm talking about are much different with these other groups.

Asians—Japanese, Chinese, Filipinos—will make very sublimated gestures. One example is a second-generation Chinese-American friend who haltingly makes eye contact. I asked him about why he looked away a lot and he replied that his Dad chided him for staring when he was young. He thought it was rude. They may stand this far away from you, and when you look them in the eyes, they may look away a little bit. You may feel that they're really being cold—"I don't think this guy likes me very much"—but that's the way they are. Even if they're second- or third-generation, they've been brought up this way.

Versus the Italians and other people from Mediterranean areas—Greece and southern France. These people do things with their hands. "The house is *this* big. You'll love it. The price is *this* big." They give directions to a taxicab, and then run alongside: "It's over there."

In 1978, I got the chance to play tennis on the European Grand Prix tennis circuit. In the semifinals of the Rome stop on the Italian Grand Prix, I played the guy who had won thirty-six consecutive tournaments in a row. His name was Guillermo Vilas. That name still rings in my head and makes me frightened even when I think about it, so you can imagine the way I felt on the court.

I got the chance to play him in the semifinal match, and I was about to win the first set of a three-set match. I was about to win that point, and I served the ball. A good way to win a point is serving the ball. I served the ball, ran up to the net, and had my racket up for the volley, but he was such a hot player, he lobbed it right over my head.

I ran back to the baseline, and we rallied baseline to baseline for about fifteen shots. On a clay-court surface, that's grueling tennis. Finally, he hit a short shot to about the midpart of my court, the service line. I ran up to the ball and hit the ball right down the line on his side. I saw the ball bounce on the line on his side away from him.

I looked to the umpire for confirmation, and the umpire stuck his finger in the air vertically, signifying it was out. I threw my racket up, and even though I hadn't won the match yet, only the first set, I was so excited. I said, "I won this round. I won a set on Vilas." Just then the umpire in the stand said, "Point, Vilas."

Vilas? What are you talking about? You think John McEnroe has a bad temper. You should have seen me that day. I was outraged. Just then a friend of mine up in the stands said, "Kerry, You got it all wrong. In Italy and Europe, *sticking your finger in the air is in and laying your hand flat* is out." He said, "The umpire motioned that your shot was good."

The whole switch-around in gestures: the one that means good in America means the total opposite in Italy and other areas. Realize when you're dealing with other people that they're showing you different gestures. Please don't feel intimidated when an Italian walks up to you and says, "Yes, what do you want to tell me?" "What did you say?" Or, when someone that is a little more sublimated, like an Asian, stands away from you and doesn't make eye contact with you very much, that doesn't mean they're cold. That's just a function of their culture.

Vilas did win that match. Later that morning, I couldn't keep anything down at all. I went out in Rome for some breakfast, and as I was walking down the sidewalk, I sat down at this old café.

I was really upset. I rubbed my fingers across my forehead. This would have showed frustration and tension to anyone who paid attention. A waitress came over to me and—I don't think she liked Americans much—said, "Hey, what do you eat?"

"I don't need this," I said. "Ma'am, all I want is two eggs and some kind words, please." I was really upset.

She left. After about five minutes, she brought back the eggs. She slapped it right down in front of me and started to walk away. As she walked away, I grabbed her dress. I said, "Ma'am, what about those kind words?"

She looked at me and said, "Don't eat them eggs."

Don't Drop It

Another thing we see is the "don't touch me" or "don't drop it" gesture. I love this one. Have you ever been walking through somebody's house, pick up a trophy, and say, "Geez, this is a beautiful trophy"? You look back at the person, and they're doing the "don't drop it" gesture by putting their hands below the possession or stepping closer just in case they have to intervene with a catch.

Or people walk up to your geranium. They want to smell it, and you get very nervous they might pull it out or damage it some way.

Here's a sign that I call "pride of possession." Remember the last time you bought a new car? You took it home, you closed the door, you locked it. You got about four or five steps away toward your house. You stopped, you looked back at your car. Isn't that a gorgeous car?

Better yet are those people who look at their cars, and as they're talking to somebody, they have their hands on the car. "Hands off, it's mine!" If the other person puts his hands on it, the owner looks at his hands. Things like that happen very often with things we're very proud of.

Headlocks and Hugging

Here's another type of gesture. Sometimes we think of relationships as exactly what people say they are, but sometimes that's not true.

Say I'm the broker, and you come in the office. We're talking, and I introduce you to my assistant. I say, "Kate is my right-hand person. Boy, without Kate, my business would go down the tubes.

To tell you the truth, if I wasn't married, I'd sure ask this little lady to marry me. She's so much help." As they say it, an arm goes around the employee with a squeeze. Perhaps even around the upper shoulders. She's such a warm person. Of course, I am married, and she's just a friend."

Sometimes we don't see the side shoulder hug, headlock routine, but we do see people being hugged. This is possessiveness. That person thinks this individual is more than just a friend. If a man does this to another man, he is indeed a very close friend.

Signs of Overconfidence

I'd like to tell you about another thing, which I fondly call the "sergeant." It's a form of overconfidence, sometimes cockiness. Have you ever shown a house to somebody who has their hands locked behind their back? They walk through the house like a drill sergeant. This person is inspecting things. They're looking for cracks. They look at wallpaper; they'll flip the wallpaper. They'll run their finger across the walls, and they'll look for dirt. They might kick a wall to find out if it's solid. They'll kick doors, they'll slam cabinets. This type of person is looking for something wrong.

This kind of individual is very difficult to deal with. If you say the house is 1256 square feet, and he finds out it's 1240, he'll call you on it. He'll say, "You lied to me once; you'll lie to me again." This person is very suspicious; he's trying to catch you in things.

Here's my favorite along the lines of overconfidence—Mr. Superiority. You interlock your hands behind your head. You pull the chair back, and you lean back in your chair. Have you ever seen somebody like this? You're talking to him, and the person looks as if he couldn't care less. You really know the person is overconfident when, after he leans back in the chair, he has his hands linked behind his head. He puts his feet up on the table in front of him.

Sometimes we like confident people, because they tend to be very decisive. Here's a way to deal with them.

Number one, find out what your client's one-, three-, and five-year goals are. Most people, especially in places like California, are very wary of real-estate people because one out of every eighteen adults in California has a real-estate license. So it's normal to be suspicious. You know you're good and I know you're good, but if these people don't know, spend time talking and developing rapport.

Here's something else. Find out what they want from a property, whether they want an investment, whether the wife needs a bigger house, whether they are trying to use it as a tax shelter. Find out exactly what their goals are, what they want from their financial goals for the next one, three, and five years, and try to appeal to them as trying to help them achieve their goals.

Who can resist that? You're trying to help someone achieve their goals. You're not trying to sell something. You're trying to be an advisor and help them in that way. Be an advisor, be a counselor. With these people, stay away from every salesy thing you've ever learned. They'll rebel against it.

Cooperation

Cooperation, or what we call enthusiasm plus, refers to people that sit on the edge of their chairs and nod their head up and down. Their pupils dilate. They smile at you as you're talking to them. You know they like you. They're interested in you. If they're cooperative and they like you, they don't have their coats buttoned. They don't have themselves dressed as if they're a cocoon.

To show honesty, they put their hands flat on their chests. They may even put their hands on their abdomen lower toward their stomach. It shows that they not only feel good about you, they feel honest towards you. They're being truthful. In this age of plasticity and phoniness, sometimes we need to know this. It's good to see words backed up by body language cues that underline their sincerity.

"You commented about that busy street being right next to your house. It's not going to keep you up at night. There aren't that many cars in the middle of the night. You won't be woken up. Trust me."

You know one other thing we see as far as these gestures go, the trust-me gesture, and people who are accepting towards us, are those individuals that touch us.

Did you ever notice that when people like you, they go up to you and touch your arm? If they want to tell you a joke, they get close to you and say, "Hey, did you hear about the lady that fell off her tricycle?" They try to reinforce that closeness.

I've Got a Secret

A related technique is called "moving closer," otherwise known as "I've got a secret."

Why do tend to believe things that we hear when we eavesdrop? You can imagine fourteen people at a swimming pool running off to make a million dollars on a hot tip they overheard some broker give to somebody else.

If you want someone's attention, whisper. If you want somebody to listen, whisper. Isn't that true?

Don't go up to your client and say, "I want you to buy this house." If you want to do something that will really have a lot of impact, walk up to your client and say, "We've been looking at this one property  for about two weeks now, and I know you've been trying to make a decision about it, and we've been doing a lot of work on it. To tell you the truth, just between you and me, the guy is a little bit desperate, and I think you can probably get the property for about $30,000 below list."

You think your client won't pay attention to that? Of course he will. I have one manager down in Mission Viejo in Southern California. When he closes somebody, he does the same thing. He says, "I've been working with you for a long time. It's $30,000 below market. I'll write up an offer right now if you want to take it."

Smiles

We use smiles in everything we do. In fact, we can tell a lot about how positively someone thinks about us by their smile.

One kind is the *lips-together smile*. People give it you to say, "I've had a wonderful time. Please come back soon. Don't call us, we'll call you."

To give you an example, in the old days when Kirby vacuum-cleaner salesmen would knock on doors, they would say, "My name is Kerry Johnson. I'm from the Kirby vacuum-cleaner company. I'd like to take this dirt in my hand right now, go in your living room, throw this dirt in your living room, and I'll take this nice, new Kirby vacuum cleaner, and I'll vacuum it up in five seconds flat. I know that when I get this done, you'll buy the vacuum cleaner."

The customer goes, "Oh, great. Dirt in my living room." This is exactly the kind of smile we see with people that don't really enjoy being with us and haven't had a good time: "What a lovely meeting we had today, but don't ever come back."

Then we have something called the *upper smile*. The upper smile shows only the upper teeth. It's a little bit better than the courtesy smile, which we give everybody whether we like them or not.

Say your spouse comes up to you and says, "Guess what. Mom's here, and this time she says she'll stay for a month."

You go, "I'm glad to hear that," and give the upper smile.

Say you're leaving someone's office; you shake hands, and that person says, "Good to see you again. I'm hoping we can meet next week," and gives this smile. It's an ambivalent smile. It means they enjoy being with you, but they didn't have a really good time.

What about those really big smiles? An old Chinese proverb says, "Beware of the man whose stomach doesn't move when he laughs, because he's probably laughing insincerely." I'd like to change that a little: "Beware of the person who doesn't smile teeth-to-teeth, because they're probably smiling insincerely too."

There are people that end conversations, and as you're ready to leave, they shake hands with you, and say, "Good to meet you. I really had a nice time." If they open their mouth and all teeth are showing, they sincerely enjoyed being with you. They felt very comfortable with you. It was a good meeting as far as they were concerned. It's an instant way to find out if they liked the meeting, if they found it was productive or not.

Defensiveness

Defensive people are tough. They're probably the most resistant you'll encounter. If someone goes into defensiveness, they're about to leave. This is the worst type of resistance you can get.

There's a lot of defensive postures such as crossing the legs, but I'm going to give you different levels of defensiveness, and I'll show you how to deal with these people too.

Have you heard that crossed arms are a defensive posture? They may or may not be. Check the temperature of the room. Is it cold? Is it hot? Maybe they're just comfortable that way. If someone has their arms crossed loosely, they may or may not be defensive, but if they cross their arms tightly, you know they're defensive. If they're gripping their arms or gripping their hands, you also know they're defensive. I call the sitting-bull posture. Just imagine a sitting bull with his legs crossed, sitting down like this.

When a person has his arms crossed with fists clenched, it's even more defensive. You can just imagine this man on an airplane. He's heard about airplane accidents. He knows every time a bolt falls off and every time they have a near-miss. This person is waiting for something fiery to fall off. He's going to be ready, so he takes that pose.

Another one along these same lines is arm gripping. Have you seen people that grab their own arms? I also call this white-knuckle

resistance. People who grab their arms when they're with you are extremely defensive. You can bet that they're not listening to you. You can bet they're thinking of ways to get away from you or of something totally opposite to what you're talking about.

I have a theory about what I call free-floating defensiveness. Every day more than 100 things happen to us that cause us to be stressful: getting cut off on the freeway, having somebody put us on hold, having a deal fall through, somebody not calling us back when they promised they would, a rep who says he can get something done for us but he never calls us back, or our broker, who schedules a meeting because we need to talk to him on Monday but comes back from his weekend on Tuesday. Little things like that can make us upset, and they can build and build, causing a high level of stress and defensiveness.

Kids sleep with their thumbs in their mouths, in a rolled-up position. Adults do something similar. They give themselves reassurance by crossing their arms. Again, please don't think that everybody who crosses their arms is defensive, but watch for other gestures that may show defensiveness too.

How many times have you seen someone leaning or turning towards the door? You're with somebody, and you're talking to them in your office. The person is leaning with their shoulders pointed toward the door. The first listen to you, but then look towards the door. This person wants to leave. It's a totally defensive posture. In fact, I even like to say that if feet are pointed towards the door of the house, usually it means the person would like to take a couple of steps.

Crossed legs, as I've said, may or may not mean defensiveness, but when the person crosses his legs tighter, that may be defensiveness. Have you seen people cross their legs, and then cross their ankles, which is what I call a double-cross? Then they cross their arms. This is a much tighter position.

My wife, Merita, is a great arm crosser. I can read her so well. If we're in the car, and if we're in an argument of any kind at all. I know that whenever she crosses her arms tightly, she will be upset at me. I ask her, "Merita, what's the matter?"

"Nothing."

"You OK?"

"Fine."

But I know something is upsetting her. Watch the next time your husband or your wife becomes upset. See what they do.

OK, application time. Here's a good way to get defensive people to open up a little bit. Whatever you're doing, stop talking. Stop selling. Stop showing. Stop doing everything. The person is about to leave. You need to save the situation.

Make sure to get the person to talk to you: "I can see you don't like the house very much, or you don't like the financing. Which is it? Is there something about it you don't quite agree with? Is there something you don't like about this? What do you think about it?"

Get the person to talk, because that's the only way you can get the person back in the conversation. If you continue, that person's going to say, "Look at the time. I have an appointment." It's the same thing I always do when I want to get away from somebody. They're out the door. It's unfortunate, but it happens quite a bit.

Nervousness

Nervousness is something we see in people who are a little insecure. They don't really feel very comfortable around us. These are also the people who feel a little bit intimidated by you. And when they're not comfortable, you do not sell them.

People do little things to show their discomfort. Number one is clearing the throat. How many times have you heard people say, "Good to meet you, ugh. My name is, ugh, Ginger"? Clearing the throat excessively is a sign of nervousness. They feel uncomfortable or nervous around you, or say, "Uh, uh, uh, you know?" "I'd like to show you this, uh, beautiful, uh, house over here. It has, uh, four bedrooms, you know?" When people say, "Uh, uh," they're so nervous they're forgetting the next thing to say. They say "uh" to give themselves time to think about what to say next.

"You know": If I go to someone and say, "Sharon, I really enjoyed the luncheon you treated me to last time I was up here, and especially the lobster, you know?" As I do that, Sharon feels compelled to go, "Yeah, huh-uh," nodding her head up and down: "Of course, keep going." People say "you know" to get reassurance, to get you to nod your head up and down so they feel more accepted by you.

Once when I saw the great motivational speaker Zig Ziglar, I said, "Zig, you know so many stories, and you're so flowing and logical and fluid whenever you're talking."

He said, "Kerry, you know, whenever I forget what I'm going to say next, I just start talking about my dog and my wife, and I start speaking a little bit more slowly until I remember what I'm going to say. Then I start talking again and going into my topic."

Sometimes people do the same thing, but it's not like the nervousness gesture, where people really need reassurance from you by saying things like "you know."

Here's another one. Ever notice when people fidget? They're moving their legs, pulling up their pants, straightening their tie, squirming in their jacket. People like this are very nervous too. Give this person some time to get used to you. Don't go into business too quickly.

Some people you can just fly into, like the person who uses the steepling gesture. You can just fly into business, and then later on you can find out about their life, what they want from a property, what their goals are for their family, their one-, three-, and five-year goals. You can be advisors to these people, but these people need to know you first. They feel very uncomfortable around you.

Another one is called *hiding conversation*. Did you ever notice when people are a little bit nervous, they cover their mouths when they talk to you, and they might look down a little bit?

A woman told me this story. When she was taking a client through an empty house, she showed the man the kitchen, showed him the bedroom, and walked over to the fireplace and said, "Isn't this a beautiful fireplace?"

Out of nowhere, he said, "You're a pretty hot-looking lady, aren't you?"

They were all alone, and she went, "Oh, thank you very much." Very embarrassed, but think: if she had projected herself—"Thank you for the compliment"—she might have given him a come-on. She was embarrassed yet appreciative, so she covered her mouth and said, "Would you like to see the front yard?" Like "give me a little more space in here."

Here's the last one in this category of nervousness: people that jingle money in their pockets. We call this "moneybags." Although this sometimes shows boredom, jingling money in the pockets usually indicates nervousness.

People who do this don't appear to be bored, but they need to do something with their hands. Just like kids: they have to do something. They squirm all over the place. They have to do something with their hands. This is along the same lines.

Interrupt Gestures

Sometimes we talk too much. People will give us little signals that they want to talk, but we go on and on, and they can't seem to get in a word in edgewise. They will put a finger up to their mouth that says, "I want to say something. Please let me talk."

There's what I call an "earful tearful." When the person grabs their ear and pulls their earlobe, this is also a cue to stop talking. The last one I'll mention is one of the most effective— touching someone on the arm.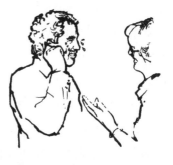

The point is, if the person is showing signs that they want to talk, please do everything you can to let them.

Suspicion and Frustration

We find suspiciousness in people when they don't quite agree with things that we're saying. Suspicious people tend to do little things that say, "Come on, you have to be kidding." One is rubbing their nose. Another is rubbing their neck. They're showing that they don't really agree with what you have to say. In this case, show them things that prove what you're talking about. Give them names and numbers.

As for frustration, probably one of the most prevalent signs is scratching the back of the head. I was in an Allstate real-estate office a few months ago. I saw a woman at the desk, and she was scratching her head like this. I walked over to her, and I said, "Is everything OK?"

She said, "Well, to tell you the truth, I just had a loan fall out. The guy couldn't qualify, and I have eight days to find another." She was scratching her head and the back of her neck. Frustration, high tension level—she was very worried. It's a good example of the frustration gesture.

Sandy and I went to Palm Springs once. I called up a number of tennis clubs, but they would not let me play because I was not a member. Sandy called up a place called the Tennis Club, which is the most prestigious club in Palm Springs.

They said, "Well, who is this guy?"

Sandy said, "He's only the most renowned tennis player in the world. He was on the European Grand Prix Circuit two years ago. He's good enough."

Sandy turned to me and said, "Hey, you got a tennis match."

"Great," I said. "I'll be there at 8:00."

The next day, the best junior player they had showed up on the court. He had his coach there. He had all his friends there. They even had a newspaper reporter who wanted to report on the match.

I just wanted to play a little friendly game of rally. I'd had a little bit too much to drink the night before, and I hadn't played tennis for a while. This kid whipped my socks off.

Between points, as he was creaming me, I found myself scratching the back of my head, thinking, "What do I have to do to beat this kid? This kid is tough. He's going to be hard to beat."

Clenched hands are another sign of frustration. Clenching hands, hand wringing—these individuals are very stressed. They're very upset. Watch out for them because they are very uncomfortable, and they're insecure about something. Go ahead and ask them, "Is everything OK? Can I help with something?" They'll usually let their hearts out to you.

The last one in this is defensive beating. People walk around tapping the back of their head. They usually also pace. They walk up and down and pace back and forth. They keep pacing.

One last thing to realize: you affect other people's gestures by the gestures that you make. When you're with a client and you have your arms crossed, what does it cause the client to feel? Defensive, doesn't it? But if you have your hands on your hips, what are you causing the client to feel? You're causing the client to feel confident too. If you talk with your hands open, you smile, you nod your head up and down, your eyes are dilated, you're receptive, you cause the person to feel more open to you.

Here's a way of controlling yourself with your gestures. Think of your last fight with your girlfriend, boyfriend, spouse. Now think of that fight again, and smile.

Keep that smile. The fight doesn't seem nearly as negative, does it? It doesn't seem like such a bad thing.

Now do the opposite. Think of the last party you went to where you had a lot of fun. Now frown. Really frown. It wasn't that good of a party, I'll tell you that.

Do you see the point? We have receptors in our skin that directly influence the way we think. What happens when you get off the phone with somebody you don't like, somebody that hangs up on you? You say, "Damn, I hate this business. I'd like to go out and get a real job."

What happens if you just smile? It doesn't seem quite as bad. Try smiling the next time you feel anxious or upset, and your outlook will be a little better. If you want to feel bad, frown while you're thinking of something nice. It'll work every time.

Gestures in Context

The gestures I'm showing you here are not meant to be read exactly as I'm describing them. A person who has their legs crossed is not necessarily being defensive, just as the individual who drops his glasses down the bridge of his nose and does the what-was-that-again gesture isn't always resistant to something you've just said. Look at these gestures in the context of the words that are being said. Also, look at the rest of their gestures. Read groups of gestures. Read gesture clusters.

You don't have to be a psychologist. You don't have to go to school for ten years to make better use of these hidden communications that I've been talking about.

Five

Persuasion as Science and Art

L ife would be a lot easier and more productive if the people we interface with saw eye to eye with us on the things that are important to us, but in reality, we must influence these people and persuade them in the direction we'd like.

Persuasion has been defined as that which causes an attitude change through the installation and implementation of ideas. In this chapter, we will be looking at what persuasion is, why it is sometimes difficult to persuade others, and some techniques you may find useful in getting a persuasive message across. Frequently we come against walls and barriers during the persuasion process. This chapter will also look at how to break down these barriers by changing attitudes.

The Bible says that Samson slew the Philistines with a jaw-bone of an ass, and unfortunately the same weapon is still used in business today. The definition of an influential and persuasive person is someone who tells the listener exactly what he wants to hear. Unfortunately, many of us don't know what the listener wants to hear. Consequently, we need to know more about how to persuade others as well as how to cause others to act on a persuasive message.

Persuading through the Senses

Two researchers from Stanford University, Richard Bandler and John Grinder, found out that people perceive information through specific senses, and are more easily persuaded through these senses.

For example, you might ask someone, "Do you understand the financing on this house?" They might say, "Yes, I *see* your point. Interesting." Or "I *hear* what you're saying," or, "I *feel* I understand."

If you appeal to the dominant sense of perception in a given individual, they'll be more easily persuaded. Let me give you an example.

If I go to Bill and I say, "Bill, do you understand what I'm talking about?" he says, "Yes, I *feel* I understand." This person is more tactically oriented. If you're a realtor showing a house, get this person to touch things. He'll be more easily persuaded by that. If you're showing a comp analysis, make a copy and give it to the person. Always let them touch something, because they'll be more easily persuaded that way.

If they say, "I *see* what you mean. I *see* your point," do the same thing. Let them see things as you're talking to them. Again, give them something to hold, something to touch.

The Four Basic Desires

In the persuasive process, some of the most important elements are the four basic interests and desires that all humans have. They are: one, for *security*; two, a desire for *acceptance*; three, for *ego satisfaction*; and four, a desire for *physical comforts*.

If you understand these elements and know how to utilize them, you will become a better persuader. You'll help the people you are influencing to act on your message even if you don't have a golden tongue or a gift of gab, or aren't a natural salesperson.

The first is security. Many salespeople realize that in order to sell a product, they must give their prospects a feeling of security when dealing with them, or give them the feeling that the salesperson is concerned with the prospect's security. The salesperson must develop trust. A famous philosopher once said, "Without trust, language is just the empty jangling of sounds." *With* trust, language can be one of the warmest and most comforting interchanges humans may have.

Recently, my secretary bought a new car. She had been to a number of different automobile dealerships and found herself in yet another one. After a short time, she realized that she wasn't going to get any better deal from one dealer or the other, so she started to leave his office.

As she was walking out, the salesman noticed the tires on the car that she wanted to trade in. He said to her, "Ma'am, I just can't let you leave here with those bad tires. In fact, I can't let you potentially harm yourself or your child by driving home on the freeway with tires like that. Those tires are so dangerous that I would feel personally responsible for letting that happen. Why don't you leave your car here, and drive that new one home today?"

That is all my secretary needed in being persuaded to buy the car from this dealer. She felt that he really had concern and empathy for her safety. He got the sale, and she went home with a new car.

In order to develop security, first you must develop rapport. You must cause the person you are persuading to be receptive by building trust and empathy in the rapport development period. In the automobile transaction, the salesman was offering the same deal as every other dealer in town, but he got the sale because he showed an interest in her security.

Acceptance

The second desire is for acceptance. We all have a deep desire for and interest in acceptance, and this manifests itself in many things that we do in our daily lives. From childhood, we all have a deep desire to be accepted by our peers. When we are young, we dress the same way as our friends do. In schools, friends in the same cliques use the same jargon and slang.

The desire for acceptance manifests itself in adults too. We buy the same toys for our children. We frequently say the same things and use the same expressions.

During the 1976 Winter Olympics, Dorothy Hamill won a gold medal in women's figure skating. She had an interesting haircut, a geometric style, with relatively straight hair. The whole world would learn to fall in love with it. Just a few months after winning the medal, thousands and thousands of other women around the world were wearing the Dorothy Hamill haircut. In Paris and New York, where designers set the fashion trend, a few of the ultrafashionable women wore them immediately, and more and more followed.

Another example is metal tennis rackets. They came into vogue with tennis players. Within a few short months of the debut of those metal rackets, almost every tennis player had one.

Another example of acceptance is the late comedian George Carlin. A friend of mind met him once in an airport in Atlanta. After speaking to him for a few minutes, he asked Carlin, "How did you ever get to be a comedian?"

Carlin answered, "That is simple to answer. I merely started out being a clown and a comic because of a deep desire for people to like me. I wanted people to see me and like me for who I am." He told my friend that many comedians start out the same way. They want to be accepted. They want to rise and have people love them.

A desire for acceptance can be used in application for the persuasive process in the form of a compliment or an expression of liking. The late Joe Girard, the self-made millionaire who sold more cars and trucks than anybody in the world, had what he called the Law of 250. He believed that everybody he sold a car to, or came in contact with, knew at least 250 people and would see them within a one-month period of time. He believed that each person he sold a car to would tell at least 250 people about Joe Girard, whether they liked his service or not. In turn, they would keep on referring other people to him, and he would soon have a huge group of prospects from that one sale.

Girard went a step further and appealed to the customer's desire for acceptance. Whenever he sold a car to someone, he found out their birth date and wedding anniversary. After the sale was consummated, he sent the buyer a card saying, "Thanks for buying a car from Joe Girard. I like you." The "I like you" represented Joe Girard's acceptance of the buyer. He would send that person a birthday card and an anniversary card. This plays on acceptance and persuasion, and it worked so well that Girard had incredible repeat sales as well as referrals.

Even if the car turned out to be the proverbial lemon, it's hard to believe that anyone who bought a car from Joe Girard wouldn't go back to him again, because he showed them that he liked them. The prospect thought of him as "good old Joe Girard" instead of "the guy I bought my car from."

Joe Gandolfo, the man from Florida who sold more life insurance than anyone else in the country, also had a method of showing acceptance. He would prospect a number of different career groups; among these, he went to workmen who mine for metals. He would drive up to a mine, meet the miners, and try to sell to them, but he realized that they would be put off and suspicious and uncomfortable if he wore his normal dress suit. So in the trunk of his car, he had a dirty old shirt and a pair of pants that had seen their better days. He rolled up the sleeves of his shirt and put his old pants on. He also wore a hardhat. He had a good hit ratio in selling to the miners because he tried to be one of them. He wanted to be accepted as well as showing the miners that he accepted them on equal terms.

Ego Satisfaction

Third, we all have an interest in and desire for ego satisfaction. We spend our lifetimes developing our egos and want to preserve them. Why do we have egos? We have them because of certain emotions. We want self-respect. We want to maintain a high self-image, and we want self-confidence. Anything that may potentially deflate the ego or damage it will meet with great defensiveness and resistance.

Many things in our daily lives cause us to be defensive. There is the theory of 100 abuses. It says that during the day, we are often not treated as we would like to be. In fact, we each have at least 100 things happening to us every day that lower our self-image and abuse our egos.

Some examples are being put on hold on the telephone for a lengthy period of time, being cut off on the freeway, having someone hang up the phone on us. With ladies, a man not opening a door for them, or someone not saying thank you after you they done something to benefit them. These things happen to each and every one of us every day. They causes us to be defensive and resistant to new things, because the unknown could potentially hurt our egos.

One example of the role that egos play in our lives is people who brag about things. All of us, from time to time, have bragged about a great feat or about something that we wanted another person to marvel a. A good example is cars.

When we buy a new car, we frequently say, "See that little red car over there? Do you know how much they wanted for it? $5,000. But I got it for $2,999. Not only am I a good negotiator, but I really knew what I was doing." What is our subconscious saying here? Psychologically, it is saying, "Look at me. I'm here. I'm important."

I recently went to a men's clothing store and was in the market for a new suit. I tried on a jacket and pants of this suit, and the salesman came over to me and said, "How do you like it?"

I replied, "Well, it's nice, but how much is it?" After he told me, I said, "I don't want to buy the whole store. I just want to buy the suit."

Then the salesman asked me what I did for a living. I told him that I was an industrial psychologist and that I travel around the country doing workshops and seminars for businesses and organizations.

The salesman said to me, "Sir, a man as important and prestigious as you needs to look the best that he possibly can. I think this suit makes you look like the important person that you obviously are."

That's all it took. I asked what the price was one more time and said, "Where do I sign?"

We have all heard the Golden Rule. "Do unto others as you would have them do unto you." I prefer to rephrase it to say, "Do unto me as I would have done unto myself." Treat me like I want to be treated. I don't want to be abused. My ego wants to be preserved.

Recently, while I was consulting for a computer corporation, I spoke to a personnel firm who was placing a man in our organization. When I called the manager of the firm on the telephone, he had an interesting way of boosting my ego. He said, "Dr. Johnson, how are you?" Then said away from the telephone, "Jenny, hold all my calls. Kerry's on the phone."

Whether the conversation was two minutes or twenty minutes long, he'd always end with something like, "Kerry, it's been a pleasure talking to you. Please call any time." Even though this may sound plastic and a little hokey to some people, I always went away from a conversation with that man feeling warm and good about myself because of this appeal to my ego. He was a great persuader, and consequently, I strongly recommended that we hire him.

Physical Comforts

The fourth of the primary interests and desires is the desire for physical comforts. Madison Avenue advertising firms deal in persuasion on a mass scale. They're saying, "We know how to solve your problems. Purchase our product." What they are doing is pushing life benefits. People buy things to satisfy their needs or perceived needs.

A good example of this is a TV commercial for a small Japanese car. A millionaire is being chauffeured in this small import to his mansion. When he gets to his estate, the chauffeur opens the door for him and asks him what he's going to do with all the money he's saved from buying the car. The millionaire looks at the chauffeur saying, "I believe I'll save that too." It makes the viewer think that if he too buys Japanese sports cars, he'll save a lot of money and become a millionaire.

Always realize that the person you're speaking to has a deep emotional desire for physical comforts. He will try anything within reason to make life happier through the acquisition of material things that will help him feel more fulfilled in life.

If you are aware of these four universal human interests and desires—security, acceptance, ego satisfaction, and physical comforts—and you appeal to a person's wants and desires for these things, the persuasion process will become a very easy and pleasant experience. No one will feel coerced or forced into any decision.

Making Use of Receptivity

In the persuasion process, we must always be aware of the importance of receptivity. Receptivity is being open and responsive to ideas and suggestions, and being willing and ready to accept those ideas. The person we are trying to persuade must be receptive to the message if he is to accept it. Receptivity must be established.

One major roadblock to receptivity is distraction. The people we are persuading must not be distracted, either from internal or external preoccupations or influences.

A common setting in which people may become very distracted is in a restaurant. One person has only a blank wall or the kitchen to focus on, while the other has a clear view of everyone who enters and exits the restaurant as well as of every move the waitresses make. Be sure to sit your client in the seat facing the wall or kitchen, and you are sure to ensure a much higher level of receptivity than if he is allowed to watch all the activity in that restaurant.

Another problem in establishing receptivity is the distance between a present attitude and the new idea you may be trying to get the person to adopt. It is much more difficult to try to get an archconservative, hard-line Republican to become a liberal Democrat than it is to ask a secretary to have lunch from 12:30 to 1:30 instead of 12:00 to 1:00. Although this seems difficult in instances when there is a great distance between attitudes, it is not impossible.

One of the most important facets of establishing receptivity is the effect that a new idea or attitude change may have on the person's ego and self-image. As we saw before, ego plays a great part in attitude change.

Back in the eighties, when computer firms were vigorously marketing business computers, many businessmen felt they did not need a business computer because they didn't feel that they had problems in their companies. Some felt the company possibly could be improved upon, they felt, but it was probably something that internal management could deal with. Consequently, many firms had trouble marketing the early computers, because management egos and high overconfidence stood in the way. It is important to realize ego position in any persuasive message, because one of the toughest things to get through in penetrating a wall or attitude barrier is the ego.

Doubt and Receptivity

Let's look at the persuasive process technically now. Questions and expressions of doubt usually indicate receptivity. Flat statements such as "That price is too high" indicate low receptivity or rejection, as opposed to an open question such as "Why should I pay your price when I can get it for 10 percent less elsewhere?"

Receptivity also increases with the degree of questioning. The comment "Why should I pay your price?" is much less receptive than "How much is it?" When someone such as a prospect makes a flat assertion in opposition to an idea, the salesperson must be careful not to cause that individual to be more defensive by allowing the conversation to lead to an argument. In order to try to persuade him, explore that person's position and try to find a weakness in his argument. Lead that person through an objective survey of his position. When you do this, you will find one of two things. One, you will find that the argument is sound, in which case it's probably a good idea to drop your attempt at a persuasive message. Or, two, you will be able to find a weak point in the argument. This may serve as an opening and as a place to insert your persuasive message.

Note too that when you encounter a roadblock in receptivity, in order to keep the individual from becoming defensive, you must withhold your argument until the other person becomes more receptive.

Years ago, the Los Angeles Dodgers played the New York Yankees. A player on the Yankee team was called out trying to steal second base. Manager Billy Martin ran onto the field and started screaming, yelling, and showing visible signs of being upset at the umpire. Although he tried to persuade the umpire he was wrong, the umpire crossed his arms in a defensive position and looked up at the sky. After a few moments, Billy Martin went back to his seat and sat down.

We frequently see examples of this in people we try to persuade. Even though they may not look up at the sky and cross their arms, they are giving us the same blank stare, and we feel as though we are speaking to a brick wall.

A real-estate manager is trying to convince an agent to spend more time prospecting through phone calls and farming (a farm is a realtor's prospecting area or location) and to take less floor time in answering the telephone in the office. The manager says, "What do you think? Do you feel that you should spend more time prospecting on the phone?"

The agent answers, "I can make better use of my time picking up requests and following up on them by phone. I don't think it is good utilization of time making cold calls. I would rather walk a neighborhood going from door to door. I may not get more people, but the prospects I get from floor time will be much more beneficial in the long run."

The weakness in this argument is the agent saying, "I may not get more prospects."

The manager takes that as his opening and inserts his message: "You need more prospects. I agree. Farming will give you more prospects. You can continue to have floor time too, but you will have more people to work with if you spend more time phoning and farming as well."

Another important point to remember is to present your ideas and promptly get feedback. Psychological studies show us that we shouldn't speak to anyone far more than twenty seconds without getting their response. After twenty seconds, there is too much information for most people to absorb and remember. Get response and feedback about how that person feels about your message. This fosters acceptance as well as enhancing the ego. It reassures the other person that their opinions are important as well as keeping communication channels open.

Another point to remember is called the *commander syndrome*. The more a person is governed by the need to prove himself, the less likely he is to be receptive to another person's logic. People with the commander syndrome need to decide on things themselves. They need to be in command. They may not be easily persuaded. Ideas must be made to seemingly come from the person they are addressed to.

An example of this is in the popular TV show *M*A*S*H*. On that show, Colonel Blake frequently thinks out loud, and while he's thinking, Corporal Radar will help him with his thoughts. In one episode, Radar comes to Colonel Blake and says, "Sir, we are almost out of medical supplies."

Colonel Blake says, "What? We're out of supplies?"

Radar has a quick solution. "Let's call up the 4076 and see if they can give us some supplies until we can order some from Tokyo."

Colonel Blake says, "I've got it. Radar, go call the 4076, and ask if we can have some medical supplies until we can order some from Tokyo."

Radar answers, "Yes, sir." Even though Radar first presented the idea, Colonel Blake presents as though it was his original idea. This need is frequently found in people who have fairly low self-esteem and a need to take credit themselves.

In situations such as this, try to give the listener the impression that you are a neutral-information broker. Give them a number of different suggestions and alternatives, such as, "Colonel Blake, we could order some supplies from Tokyo, which may take two weeks, we could get interim supplies from the 4076, or we can shut down part of our hospital due to lack of supplies." In this case it becomes obvious that borrowing the supplies is the best solution.

Giving a choice to an individual like this will help him feel as though the decision was all his, and as a result he will be much happier with it, with the added advantage of preserving his ego. If the individual picks the wrong avenue or becomes negative, offer additional information and ask him to reevaluate, but by all means, do not try to convince this individual that your way is the only right one.

The law of free-floating receptivity will usually prevent any roadblocks or defensiveness from coming up. It will also maintain a high level of respect from you with the people you work with. This law dictates that the more positive people feel towards you, the more receptive they will be toward your suggestions. As a result, it will be much easier to persuade them.

A working knowledge of persuasion techniques will help anyone from managers to salespeople at all levels of business as well as in their personal lives to become better communicators and get their message across.

Persuasive people are often described as "successful" or "winners." They typically are impressive people who command high salaries, because they are able to get a message across, make it believable, and have it accepted by other people.

Persuasion is a technique that everyone needs to master. Understanding the four interests and desires—security, acceptance, ego satisfaction, and physical comforts—will allow the persuader to gain more receptivity for other people.

Six

Eight Steps to Good Listening

L istening is probably one of the most important but most mis-understood facets of communication. In this chapter, we will look at what listening is, why we listen the way we do, and how we can improve our listening skills.

Think back for a moment about the past week. How many people can you remember that were good listeners, people who not only were attentive, but also remembered what you said? Chances are, you only met a couple of people that you thought of as good listeners. What were your feelings towards those few good listeners? Probably ones of comfort, trust, and likability.

We are all vulnerable to certain myths about listening. Salesman very often think of themselves as being good talkers instead of good listeners. They may think of a good salesman as having the gift of gab. "He's a born salesman!" "What a promoter!" "He sure is quick on his feet!"

Are these comments focused on listening? Of course not. The focus is on talking. These people believe that selling is telling or telling is selling. They believe that speech is power and that listening is subservient to that power. Just the opposite is true: A good listener has much more power in a conversation. He is gleaning more information. In fact, when you think about a conversation when one person is talking and the other is listening, who is really directing that discussion? Isn't it the person who asks the questions? Isn't it the listener? The listener has the ability to change the subject, direct the depth or detail the speaker goes into, and even terminate a discussion entirely.

Over 50 percent of a manager's job revolves around listening. Successful and productive managers will agree. The Sperry Rand Corporation learned this too. They were purchased by Unisys, which was in turn purchased by another conglomerate, but the old Sperry Rand spent thousands of dollars training their salespeople on becoming better listeners. Their TV commercials advertised, "We have found that people just don't listen. We at Sperry are becoming better listeners. We are training secretaries to chairman of the board to listen in order to help you." These advertisements aired coast-to-coast, especially after football games. They showed salespeople, managers, and support personnel in classrooms listening to their teachers talk about listening. You could see them tilting their heads and taking notes. They were very quiet and obviously paying attention. Sperry Rand was trying to show the public that they cared about their clients and that they were willing to listen and pay attention.

This message took advantage of the emotions we feel towards good listeners, but business is not the only place where listening is important. Marriage counselors will confirm that couples break up not because of incompatibility or disagreements but because of a lack of communication.

I saw a movie about a couple who went to a marriage counselor because of strained marital relations. The counselor said, "Communicate better, and you will help your marriage. Listen to each other once in a while, and you'll be surprised at how much better your relationship will become."

The morning after seeing that counselor, the husband was reading the paper. The wife was reading another section of the paper, about fashion. The husband blurted out, "Look at that. They won again by three touchdowns. I made a pretty penny on that game."

The wife picked up on that comment and said, "A pretty penny. Look at the money I can save on this dress. If I could just get down to Saks before 1:00, I'll probably beat the crowd and get what I want. I can save a lot of money on that beautiful maroon dress that would go so nicely with my white jacket."

The husband said, "Imagine, advertising coats in the sports section. Why don't they leave them out and just put sports in it? Why do they have to let those dumb advertisements clutter up the section?"

The wife picked up on that and said, "Coats. Look at that coat. That jacket would look so good with my blue top and white belt. I have to take advantage of this sale today."

The husband put his paper down right at that moment and said, "Isn't it incredible how well we're getting along now?"

How well were they getting along? They were talking about two totally different subjects.

How much of this do you do in speaking to your spouse or loved one? Do you really listen? No one is born with the ability to listen effectively. Like all other communication skills, good listening must be learned. To a great extent this involves forming good listening habits and breaking bad habits.

Here's a short test that, if answered honestly, will give you an idea of whether you have any bad listening habits. Answer yes or no to each question.

1. You think about four times faster than a person usually talks. Do you use this excess time to think about other things while you're keeping track of the conversation?

2. Do you listen primarily for facts rather than ideas when someone is speaking?

3. Do you avoid listening to things you feel will be too difficult to understand?

4. Can you tell from a person's appearance and delivery that he won't have anything worthwhile to say?

5. When someone is talking with you, do you try to make him think you're paying attention when you're not?

6. Do certain words or phrases prejudice you so that you cannot listen objectively?

7. Do you turn your thoughts to other subjects when you believe the speaker will have nothing interesting to say?

8. When you're listening to someone, are you easily distracted by outside sights and sounds?

9. When you're puzzled or annoyed by what someone says, do you try to get the question straightened out immediately, either in your own mind or by interrupting the speaker?

10. Do you catch yourself concentrating in a conversation more on what you're going to say when it's your turn to speak than on what the speaker is saying?

Your score indicates how good a listener you are. If you truthfully answered no to all these questions, you are a rare individual and perhaps a perfect listener. You may also be kidding yourself. Every yes means you are guilty of one of the ten bad listening habits. If you scored less than 50 percent on this test, you are in the average category. If you scored better than 50 percent, you are above average.

If you did score all correct—that is, answered all no—or if you scored nine correct, you have probably either taken a listening course before or you've read about listening and are implementing these habits in your daily life. Congratulations. If you failed to score ten, this chapter can be very valuable to you, because a great part of your day is spent listening.

In business, approximately 5 percent of our day is spent writing, 15 percent is spent reading, 30 percent is spent talking, and 50 percent is spent listening. It's not surprising that so many of us are not good listeners.

Most of us have spent at least twelve years in school. During that time, we spent approximately half of our education learning to communicate. Of that time, 40 percent was spent learning how to read, 35 percent spent learning how to write, 25 percent spent learning how to talk, and only 0 to 1 percent of our time that was spent learning how to communicate was spent on learning how to listen. Much of that listening time was in the form of "Be quiet, Tommy, and pay attention," or "If you don't listen, I'll put you in the corner." A great way to learn, huh?

A few years ago, the New York City Police Department did a study of the type of men who engaged prostitutes. They found that over 36 percent of the men who went to prostitutes did so not because they were mentally deranged or had psychological problems but because they wanted someone to listen to them. They frequently would pay a prostitute just to sit and listen.

Here are some techniques and tips that will allow you to become both a better listener and a more effective and efficient communicator.

First, a good listener will repeat and clarify information. A great deal of information is lost through one-way communication. For example, a superior gives you a command: "I want you to get this out by next Monday, so see what you can do with it. Be sure it is double-spaced, and try to give the client a feeling of warmth. Make sure, above all, that you write down the price; let him know that we are going to do a good job for him." This is one-way communication. Information is lost because the listener is not participating in or clarifying the message. This is common in business and results in frequent misunderstandings.

Two-way communication is much better. When someone makes a comment or request—"See what you can do with this proposal. Try to make it as exacting as possible"—in two-way communication, the listener will say, "What exactly do you want me to do with it? When do you want it completed?" He will work with the speaker in trying to put the most information to use in the best way.

There is also a deeper facet of communication that is important in listening. It's called *congruency*. Congruency is a two-way communication involving not only interacting with a speaker, but trying to understand what the speaker is saying by listening to emotions and reaching a point of trust with the speaker.

Many of us in sales deal with the same types of people day in and day out. I met a real-estate agent recently who told me about a couple who wanted to buy a house. The couple told the agent exactly what they wanted, but the agent didn't adequately listen and consequently showed them things they didn't like.

After spending two weeks looking at the wrong kind of houses, the agent lost his clients because he assumed they were like everyone else who wanted a three-bedroom, two-bathroom home in Southern California. In order to reach congruency, a good listener will repeat and clarify information but will also summarize points at the end for the speaker.

This is important not only to let the speaker know that are you listening but also to reach the same understanding of the conversation as the speaker had intended. A good listener will repeat and clarify information.

Second, a good listener listens to a speaker at-tension, spelled AT-TENSION. During my stress workshops, I teach that stress is usually measured on a bell-shaped curve of zero to ten. Zero is a very relaxed state, almost asleep, and ten is a state of being so anxious and upset that we find it difficult even to think logically. At ten, we also have trouble concentrating on work.

On this scale of zero to ten, there is an optimal area for listening tension: the three to four level. This is where enthusiasm thrives. You feel good, and there is just enough stress to cause us to produce and achieve. When we are at that level, we are able to assimilate a lot of information that we may put into future action. When we keep ourselves very attentive, our memory improves.

A short time ago, a life-insurance agent told me that he would make referral calls. He would spend every Monday, Wednesday, and Friday mornings on the phone. One day, after about the twelfth call, he spoke to one man for a few minutes and found himself drifting off. It was brought abruptly to his attention when the prospect said, "What do you think of that, Charlie?"

The agent replied, "Right, yes, yes. Uh, I agree," even though he hadn't heard what the prospect said. A very embarrassing situation.

A good way to keep yourself attentive, to gain more information, and to be a better listener is to keep alert and grip the edge of the chair or buy a gripper that bodybuilders use.

Another thing you can do is stand up. When you stand up while you're talking on the telephone or when speaking with somebody, you cause yourself to be more alert and aware. Studies have shown that the more attentive and alert you are, the more information you will retain.

When I was an instructor at the University of California, I would suggest ways for my students to prepare for examinations. I recommended that if they walked up and down the dormitory halls reading their notes out loud or even just walking and reading them silently, they would increase their memory retention and become more efficient in studying for tests.

Being attentive, keeping yourself at that three to four stress level, and not being anxious while not being too relaxed helps increase pulse rate and increases attention span as well as helping you become a better listener. A good listener listens to a speaker *at-tension*.

Third, a good listener exchanges information. Any salesperson knows that you can't sell unless you find a need, and you can't fill it unless you ask a question about that need. Needs have to be uncovered, and the important thing is knowing how to ask questions. A good listener knows this. He doesn't ask too many questions. He doesn't give the speaker a feeling of being pumped by asking a lot of questions one right after the other.

Once I was traveling from Long Island to New York City on a commuter train. I sat next to a man who was reading a newspaper. Across from us was another man, who looking out the window at the scenery along the tracks. The man who was looking at the scenery turned to the man with the newspaper and said, "Hey, buddy, what's on the front page today?"

The newspaper reader said, "Looks like the Jordanians are having verbal disputes with the Israelis about the West Bank again. The Egyptians are reaching agreement, fortunately, about the Sinai, and it looks like it will be good for Middle East peace."

The other man said, "What about sports? How are the Knicks doing?"

"The Knicks lost last night, and it also looks like the Jets have no chance in the playoffs this year."

"What about economics?"

"The prime rate is increasing another point, and unfortunately, it looks like we're going to have a housing crisis in the next six months."

"Oh, really? What about the current fiscal crisis in New York City?"

After that, the reader crackled his newspaper, straightened it out, and put it up between himself and the person who was asking all the questions.

Can you imagine how you would feel if someone were machine-gunning questions at you like that? It's important to give prospects or anyone else you're speaking with the reason why you want to know something. Even give them past experiences.

If you tell them what you want to know and why you want to know, you will greatly enhance your chances of getting the right and appropriate information willingly from the speaker. You also develop trust and empathy with the other person if you ask a question and then give some background information about it. It will keep them from getting the feeling of being pumped or interrogated. A good listener exchanges information.

Fourth, a good listener adjusts to emotion-laden words. We all have a holding tank of works that trigger emotions. These are words which, when heard, cause us to stop listening and focus on that word during the conversation. Here are some words which may serve as examples to show you how distracting emotional words can be.

What do you think of when I say *inflation*? How about *bills*? Here are a couple more: *cost of living* and *vacation*. How about *foreign policy*? All these words conjure up opinions or emotions. Consequently, they also tend to distract the listener.

Recently, I saw an Abbott and Costello movie. Abbott was locked in a cell with a man who had a beard down to his waist and hair down to his shoulders. He was dressed in a tattered robe, and he looked as if he had been in the cell for years and years. He was obviously demented. Abbott was thrown in the cell, and he looked at his fellow prisoner and looked out the bars at the ocean.

Abbott said, "Why am I here? I've done nothing wrong. This is really going to spoil my vacation to Niagara Falls."

The madman woke up and said, "Inch by inch, slowly I turn, closer and closer . . ." and proceeded to throw Abbott against the wall of the cell and beat him up.

Abbott recovered and said, "Why did you do that?"

The madman said, "Do what? Let me help you up." He had forgotten everything he had just done.

Abbott said, "Boy, don't you ever do that to me again." He looked out the window again and said, "If only I could be in Niagara Falls right now, everything would be OK."

Suddenly the madman went into his trance again—"Inch by inch, slowly I turn, closer and closer . . ."—and again proceeded to beat up Abbott.

Abbott again shook himself out of a stupor and said, "I understand now why you did that."

The madman said, "Did what?"

"Beat me up. I know why you did it. It's because I said—"

"Said what?"

"Oh no, I'm not going to say those words again."

"What words? What are you talking about?"

"You're not going to get me to say it that easy. Oh, no."

The madman said, "I don't know what you're talking about. What is this?"

Abbott said, "You're not going to get me to say *Niagara Falls*."

"Inch by inch, slowly I turn . . ." said the madman, and the same thing happened again.

This is an example of emotion-laden words in an extreme form. A good way to avoid falling into the problems that these words bring is to try to identify with the speaker about the reason he's using the word. See the usage of that word from his point of view instead of reacting to it from your point of view. Avoid associating your own emotions with these words.

I heard a story about a college student who wrote a letter to her parents. Her mom went to the mailbox and brought the letter into the house. The father saw the envelope and said, "Sweetheart, Donna doesn't write many letters to us. I wonder what she's written about. She's probably written to tell us that she is getting bad grades and wants money."

The mother opened the letter and read it out loud to the father: "Dear Mom and Dad," the letter said. "I just want to tell you that everything is OK, and I love you both very much, but there are a couple of things I need to tell you. Something bad has happened.

"My roommate did so poorly on her midterms that she went up on top of the dorm and jumped off, committing suicide. I can't tell you how upset I was and still am. I was so depressed that I had to quit my job, and in not working, I lost my car because I couldn't make the payments.

"I still am shaken horribly over these things. Since I haven't been making any money, I moved in with my boyfriend. I know how you feel about living with a man out of wedlock, Mom and Dad, but he is such a wonderful person. He does everything for me. He gives me so much, and he doesn't even care that I'm pregnant. He says, 'Have the baby, and I'll still live with you.'

"He's such a wonderful person, Mom and Dad. He even said that he wouldn't go to the pool halls while I'm pregnant and gamble on billiards as he did before. He'll stay with me in the evenings, he says. I realize that this may not be exactly what you want for me, but he said as soon as I have the baby, I can quit school and work to support the family."

You can imagine the shock that the parents were feeling at this point. The letter went on: "Mom and Dad, none of the things I've written above are true. I love you very much and miss you, and I just wrote to say that I got a D in history and I need $100 for a ski trip next month. Love, Donna."

Can you hear all the emotional despots in words like *pregnancy, living together, suicide* that the parents focused on while reading the letter? If we are going to be good listeners, it's important to listen to the words that are being used from the speaker's point of view. A good listener adjusts to emotion-laden words.

Number five, a good listener hears the speaker out. All of us intensely dislike being interrupted. We desire to express complete ideas. We all want to be heard and desire to say what we have on our minds. It disturbs us not to be able to complete an idea or express a whole opinion.

Recently, a life-insurance agent who had previously been at one of my workshops on listening came to me and said, "Hearing a speaker out really does help. I'm in for three hours with a prospect and showed the man a life-insurance policy which would have helped him very much. Two days later, I called him back before I went to his house to deliver the policy, and the prospect said over the phone, 'I'm glad you called, Tom. I've been thinking about this policy and all the things we have talked about. I think that it isn't such a great idea for me to buy this at this time. I really don't have the money for the monthly premiums, and I'm not sure I'm ready for it anyway.'"

The life-insurance agent felt like saying, "Wait a minute. I spent three hours with you the other evening, and we talked about definite plans and advantages, the way to cope with taxes, financial planning, estate planning, and ways of building security for your family. How can you back out of something like this? You know it's the right thing for you to do, don't you?"

But the agent remembered my seminar and didn't say that. He'd learned to let the speaker complete his ideas. The prospect went on to say, "Yes, I really can't afford it, but then again, it will help my family, especially if something happened to me, and it will help with taxes. I think it's a good idea, after all. Bring the policy over, and I'll sign it."

How many times do we make mistakes by cutting in on a speaker? Find out what the speaker is trying to say first. When the time comes for you to respond to what he has said, let the speaker catch his breath before speaking or replying. This gives the speaker the idea that you are not only listening but are also thinking about your response, so it doesn't sound as if you are commenting too quickly. A good listener hears the speaker out.

Number six, a poor listener listens to facts. A good listener listens to emotions. Think of communication as an iceberg. All of the iceberg that's above water is facts. Theoretically, 20 percent is strictly facts; 80 percent of that iceberg is emotion. The 80 percent down below the waterline is the feelings and the emotions that we all have and put into every thought. If you're not listening to the whole iceberg in a conversation, you're missing 80 percent of what the person is actually trying to say.

An example of that is the common greeting "How are you?" "How are you?" is so overused that many of us automatically find ourselves responding, "Fine, great, OK," even though we haven't thought about our answer.

The person asking, "How are you?" usually doesn't care to hear how we are, but think of this as an example. If you say, "How are you?" to someone, and they say, "Great," the intonation in their voice gives you a good idea of their emotions, but are they really doing great? Do they really feel great? Is everything working out for them?

If you care, you will listen for these things, and a simple question of "How are you?" will give you a good idea of what they are really thinking. Again, try to picture yourself saying the same words that the speaker is saying. What would you be thinking if you said those words in the same way?

In asking a question of someone such as, "How is that movie?" or, "How was your vacation?" if the answer sounds superficial, if they say, "Great, wonderful, couldn't have had a better time," if they sound superficial like that, probe deeper. Try to listen for emotions. A poor listener listens to facts; a good listener listens to emotions.

Seventh, a good listener prepares for a conversation. A psychological framework is needed to orient the listener to a previous conversation. Psychological studies have shown us that memory plays a large part in listening. Not only are we able to focus better on a conversation when we remember the previous discussions, but it also helps us to avoid distractions in listening. We're able to focus on the current conversation instead of trying to recall a previous one.

A good tip for this is to have an outline of things you have talked about during any previous conversation. It also gives you a good idea of what further questions to ask and allows you to put information into a logical and flowing framework for ready referral.

Still, it is very important to keep eye contact with the speaker. Taking your eyes off the speaker and looking at a page while you take notes on what's being said or refer to notes from a previous conversation is not only discourteous, but will tend to dampen and interrupt the conversation. It is very important to jot short notes instead of writing long, drawn-out dissertations on what is being said.

Remember also that we cannot do two things at once. Psychologically it is very difficult to engage in more than one activity such as watching TV while reading the newspaper at the same time. Listening to the radio while trying to listen to someone else can result in a loss of comprehension of both.

We have a resource pool of attention in our minds that we use in listening. That resource pool is taken up by things that we are listening to, and even though we can drive an automobile and at the same time listen to something else, because we are using two different senses, hearing should involve only one input at one time.

When you speak to someone and you have had a prior conversation with that person, put the notes in front of you when you talk to that individual again. It will help you stick to the point and make you much more efficient. It will also take less time to accomplish more things during the discussion. A good listener prepares for a conversation.

Number eight, a good listener adjusts thought speed to speech speed. We listen at approximately 200 words per minute. We think four times that fast. Unfortunately, a poor listener can't adjust. We think in pictures and speak in words, and we have to encode and decode all the things that are being said into pictures and decode them out of pictures and into words.

Physiologically, we can't speak as fast as we think, and a poor listener tends to drift off and become distracted. Many times he becomes bored with a conversation that is not going very quickly and rapidly, especially if it isn't on a subject that the speaker loves.

I spoke to a manager recently who was not very articulate, succinct, or concise in his thinking. I remember him describing his current profit picture for the quarter, and he said, "Well, uh, Kerry, we're not, uh, looking very good this, uh, quarter, but, um, I think that in the, uh, long run for the, uh, year we may spurt out of this, um, slump we're, uh, having. Well, I think it will look better for us, uh, later."

I started getting bored listening to him. I found myself drifting off. Not only was he failing to keep my attention, he wasn't even speaking at a rate of 200 words a minute. I was thinking more than four times as fast as he was speaking and drifting off to a totally different subject.

When you encounter people who speak like this, or when you feel that you are daydreaming during a conversation, try to anticipate what the speaker is going to say next. If you anticipate the next point, and if you guess right, you're way ahead of the game. If you guess wrong, you still have kept yourself attentive enough to listen to the person and hear whether he's saying.

Mentally summarize what has been said up to the existing point, and try to summarize in your own mind all the points that have been made. Keep a mental bank of the main ideas the speaker has given. Try to remember what both of you have said during the conversation.

To summarize:

1. A good listener will repeat and clarify information.
2. A good listener listens to a speaker *at-tension*.
3. A good listener exchanges information.
4. A good listener adjusts to emotion-laden words.
5. A good listener hears the speaker out.
6. A poor listener listens to facts; a good listener listens to emotions.
7. A good listener prepares for a conversation.
8. A good listener adjusts thought speed to speech speed.

Being a good listener takes work and practice. One great philosopher said, "It's not that we should all be great communicators; we should be less feeble communicators."

In our highly sophisticated society, those of us who listen well tend to be more successful and tend to get much more done. Be a good listener. It'll help you in business and in your private life. God gave us two ears and only one mouth. Maybe we shouldn't try to outsmart our maker.

CPSIA information can be obtained
at www.ICGtesting.com
Printed in the USA
JSHW032323150222
22981JS00005B/142